Market Structure, Corporate Performance and Innovative Activity

PAUL A. GEROSKI
London Business School

CLARENDON PRESS · OXFORD
1994

Oxford University Press, Walton Street, Oxford OX2 6DP
Oxford New York
Athens Auckland Bangkok Bombay
Calcutta Cape Town Dar es Salaam Delhi
Florence Hong Kong Istanbul Karachi
Kuala Lumpur Madras Madrid Melbourne
Mexico City Nairobi Paris Singapore
Taipei Tokyo Toronto
and associated companies in
Berlin Ibadan

Oxford is a trade mark of Oxford University Press

Published in the United States
by Oxford University Press Inc., New York

British Library Cataloguing in Publication Data
Data available

Library of Congress Cataloging in Publication Data
Geroski, Paul.
  Market Structure, Corporate performance, and Innovative activity /
Paul A. Geroski.
  Includes index.
  ISBN 0-19-828855-7
  1. Technological innovations—Economic aspects—Great Britain.
I. Title.
HC260.T4G47 1994 94-22700
338'.064'0941—dc20

10 9 8 7 6 5 4 3 2 1

Typeset by Graphicraft Typesetters Ltd., Hong Kong
Printed in Great Britain on acid-free paper by
Biddles Ltd., Guildford and King's Lynn

For John and Andreas

Contents

List of Figures

List of Tables

1 Introduction

This book is about the causes and consequences of innovative activity. In particular, it addresses four questions which have long attracted the interest of economists: Does the structure of product markets affect the pace of innovative activity? What are the effects of innovative activity on market structure? How large a contribution does innovative activity make to productivity growth? And how does innovative activity affect corporate performance?

These are important questions because they help to inform a wide range of public and business policy choices. In the area of competition policy, the Schumpeterian debate about the effect of monopoly on innovation has raised the possibility that anti-trust actions designed to reduce static misallocations of resources may undermine dynamic efficiency, reducing welfare in the long run. This same issue arises in the design of industrial and technology policies, where policy-makers have tried to reconfigure market structures to stimulate innovativeness, experimenting with 'national champions', using procurement policies to strengthen certain client firms and tinkering with the structure of patent laws. Lying behind these initiatives is a widely held feeling that firm size is a source of competitive strength, that large firms are more able and, therefore, more likely to innovate. These ideas have also influenced the design of business policy. Many managers view size as a cause (rather than as a consequence) of competitive strength, and many worry that 'too much' competition will undermine the innovative vigour of their sectors. More broadly, debates about why the UK economy (and that of some other advanced industrial nations) seems to have lost its innovative drive often raise questions about why managers do not choose to invest more in R. & D., and many of the answers which have been proposed turn on the proposition that managers are 'too short-sighted' and underestimate the effects that innovation has on the performance of their companies.

The book is built up from a series of published empirical studies that all draw upon the same data on innovative activity, and they have been reprinted here with only very minor modifications. The individual studies were conceived and carried out independently over a seven- or eight-year period, and they do not add up to a comprehensive examination of the questions raised above. However, considered as a group, they do touch many important bases, and the use of the same data on innovative activity eliminates many of the difficulties one ordinarily has in comparing and evaluating different studies of the causes and consequences of innovation. Pulling them together in one volume, then, ought to lead to some useful conclusions about the relationship between innovation, market structure, and corporate performance.

The plan is as follows. We start in Chapter 2 with a discussion of the innovations data that will be used throughout the book. The goal is to introduce the reader to the strengths and weakness of the data, and to highlight some of the properties of the data which other scholars have uncovered. Chapters 3 and 4 examine the effects of innovation on the evolution of market structure, and the effects of market structure on the determinants of innovation. These studies examine a number of the core strands of the Schumpeterian hypothesis, and they are followed in Chapter 5 by a study which uses a less conventional methodology to explore complementary hypotheses about the relationship between entry and innovativeness. As a group of three, they contain pretty much all that this book has to say about the relationship between market structure and innovativeness. The following four chapters consider the relationship between innovation and economic performance. Chapters 6 and 7 contain two closely related studies of the effect that innovation has on productivity growth in different industries, while Chapters 8 and 9 examine the relationship between innovative activity and corporate performance measured in terms of both profitability and growth. Chapter 10 contains a summary of the more interesting and important results uncovered by these studies, and offers some broader reflections on the light which they cast on a number of public and business policy issues.

I have incurred numerous debts while doing the individual studies and in putting them together into this book, debts which a mere 'thanks' cannot repay. Three of the papers in this volume are the result of joint work, but the contributions made by Richard Pomroy, Steve Machin, and John van Reenan to the whole extend far beyond the individual chapters which they co-authored. Keith Pavitt at the Science Policy Research Unit at the University of Sussex, Paul Stoneman at the University of Warwick, John Scott at Dartmouth University, Steve Klepper at Carnagie Mellon University, Steve Davies at the University of East Anglia, Mike Scherer at Harvard University, and Dennis Mueller at the University of Maryland have all helped this work along in many ways with their useful comments and friendly support. The individual studies in the book have been presented to numerous seminar audiences over the years, and all of them bear the imprint of many helpful comments, useful discussions, and expressions of support. Last but by no means least, Christine VanderNoot put the whole thing together, and got it ready for the printers.

Despite all of these debts, I would, however, like to dedicate this book to two individuals who had absolutely nothing to do with any of the work reported here, namely John Geroski, my father, and Andreas Sampson Geroski, my son. I know that much of what I do is a complete mystery to them, but I would like them to feel that they are, and have always been, an important part of the show.

2 The SPRU Innovations Database

1. *Introduction*

The traditional methodology of those interested in studying the causes and consequences of innovative activity is the case-study, and the tools typically used by students of innovation and technological change are those of the historian and not those of the statistician. There is much to be said for this approach, as there is for good case-study work in general. The problems with it, however, are lack of generalizability and selectivity: single cases are too small a sample to support generalizations about many phenomena of interest, and they are, in any case, unlikely to be randomly chosen (most case-studies are undertaken because some special feature of the case interests the investigator). The degree to which these problems should be regarded as a set of serious drawbacks to case-study work is not, however, entirely clear. After all, if every innovation is, in some sense, unique, then each case is not so much a sample as it is the population.

The alternative to case-study work is to use a more quantitative methodology (such as econometric analysis). Although this approach has many well-known virtues, the choice between the two methodologies is not always straightforward. Case-studies provide detail and nuance, while econometric studies usually only identify broad or average tendencies in the data. Indeed, it is often almost impossible to explore the finer aspects of different hypotheses about the behaviour of agents with the kinds of structural models and estimation techniques

I am obliged to both Keith Pavitt and John van Reenen for help in interpreting the data, and for helpful comments on an earlier draft. John conducted a helpful analysis of how the times-series properties of the data may have been affected by way the data were collected, and I have drawn on some of his ideas and conclusions in Section 3. Paul Stoneman and Peter Swann also made helpful comments on an earlier draft of the chapter. The usual disclaimer applies however.

which econometricians typically use. Perhaps a more fundamental difference between case-study and econometric work is that the two methodologies necessarily draw on different populations of innovations, or focus on different types of innovative activity. To get enough data to do serious econometrics, one has to focus on a fairly broad population of innovations. There are simply not enough fundamental innovations around to collect a decent-sized sample, and it is hard to imagine any kind of structural model with parameters that can plausibly be taken as invariant across enough of them to be estimable. This means that econometric work has to focus mainly on major or, more likely, on minor innovations. Case-studies, by contrast, are most useful when the sample is the population, and this means that they are most informative when they concentrate on fundamental innovations, or on a cluster of related major innovations.

It follows from this that it is the questions which one wishes to address which are the ultimate determinants of the appropriate mix of case-study and econometric work which one ought to employ. In this book, we are interested in the relationships between innovation, market structure, and corporate performance. The innovations which are of interest are, therefore, those which are 'regularly' produced by firms, those that affect their market position on a year-by-year basis. Some of these are likely to be major innovations (e.g. the development of anti-ulcer drugs), while others will be more minor (e.g. ball-point pens). Fundamental innovations (e.g. developing the microchip), however, are likely to have very large and unusual effects on market structure and corporate performance, and they can (arguably) be set aside for special (i.e. case-study) investigation. The questions we propose to ask in this book relate to average tendencies which manifest themselves in a wide range of settings, and the answers to them are designed to create presumptions, not hard and fast conclusions. We are, for example, interested in the relationship between market structure and innovative activity. Although it is almost certainly the case that some monopolists are very innovative and others are rather sleepy, we hope that our statistical work will identify the behaviour of a bench-mark (or 'typical') monopolist that will be useful in putting more extreme cases of monopoly behaviour into proper perspective. All of this points to a methodology that is heavily tilted towards econometric work, and that is the course which we have pursued here.

The population of innovations that we will work with in what follows is rather special, and our goal in this chapter is to identify its salient characteristics. We start in Section 2 by considering the measurement of innovation in a very general way. Much of the literature which has been concerned with the relationship between innovation, market structure, and corporate performance has worked with a variety of different measures of innovation, and this has made it difficult to compare the results of different studies. In particular, it turns out that the choice of measure can have a big effect on the kinds of results that one obtains. The data that we shall use is drawn from a study of major innovations produced in the UK during the post-war period, and its sample design is the subject of Section 3. This particular data-set has two rather unusual properties which have excited some attention in the literature, and it is important to keep them in mind when interpreting the results. The first property is that very few of these innovations were first used by the firm that produced them, while the second is that small firms produced a large share of these innovations. Both of these properties of the data are discussed in Section 4, while Section 5 contains a brief summary of the discussion.

2. *Measures of Innovative Activity*

Quantitative studies of the causes and consequences of innovative activity have often been stymied by the difficulty of measuring 'innovation', and, despite its importance, empirical work in the field is, as a consequence, relatively underdeveloped. The three measures which have been used most often are: R. & D. expenditures (or the number of scientists and engineers employed in R. & D. labs), patent counts, and counts of major or minor innovations. All three have a number of virtues and a number of shortcomings (for a good discussion of the relative merits of these measures, see Cohen and Levin, 1989, and Patel and Pavitt, 1993).

R. & D. expenditures measure inputs to the innovation process. They are, however, likely to be inherently noisy measures of the output of the innovative process whenever the productivity of R. & D. varies between firms or across sectors. Further, R. & D. is not obviously an essential input into the production of innovations: plenty of firms have introduced major and minor innovations despite the lack of a formal R. & D. lab or a specific accounting of R. & D. expenditures. Finally, it may not be the annual flow of R. & D. which matters so much as the services which arise from the accumulated stock of knowledge, something which may not closely match patterns of R. & D. spending (e.g. see Griliches, 1979). Patents protect ideas rather than goods, and are, therefore, often thought of as a measure of intermediate output in the innovative process. It is generally believed that they are more highly correlated with research inputs than with innovative output (for an interesting discussion of this issue, see Griliches, 1990), and they are likely to be a noisy measure of innovative output whenever the propensity to patent varies across firms or sectors. Further, the value of individual patents varies widely, and this often makes patent counts seem like a collection of apples and oranges (for some observations on the inferences which can be drawn from data on patent counts of widely different values, see Swann, 1993).

By contrast, innovation counts have the great virtue of concentrating attention on the output of the innovative process, and, as a consequence, they are the natural measure to use in examining the causes and consequences of innovative activity. However, samples of innovations are expensive to collect, and they suffer from two interrelated problems: the unit of measurement used and selectivity. To make a unit of measurement meaningful, one needs to ensure that like is being compared with like, so that a count of two truly means twice as much innovative output as a count of one. Since this is difficult to do in general, many studies try to concentrate on collecting samples of innovations of similar importance (e.g. 'major' innovations). While this helps to solve the units of measurement problem, it creates problems of selectivity, since information about total innovative activity (e.g. 'minor' innovations that are not included in the data) is being neglected. How serious a problem this is is hard to gauge, since effects of selectivity depend on the relationship between included and omitted innovations. If 'major' innovations are the crest of a wave which brings a wave of minor innovations along with them, then variations in counts of major innovations will directly reflect variations in total innovative activity. If, on the other hand, major and minor innovations are substitute activities, then no obvious pattern may exist between variations in the output of major innovations and in total innovative output.

Whatever their particular virtues, all of these measures of

innovative activity are likely to give rise to problems of measurement error. At the very least, this will lead to some imprecision in estimates, and, therefore, to some difficulty in making
precise inferences about the point values of particular parameters of interest. However, measurement errors can also give
rise to two more serious problems: they may lead one to mis-
state the consequences of innovative activity, and they may
induce a spurious positive correlation between firm size or
market structure on the one hand and innovative activity on
the other. Five specific types of measurement errors seem particularly worrying in this context: spillovers from rivals' innovative activities, allocating the returns to innovation between
innovation producers and innovations users, omitting unsuccessful innovations, correcting for variations in 'technological
opportunity', and firm-size biases which arise in the construction of the data. We consider each in turn.

The proposition that measurement errors may lead to biased
estimates of the effects of innovation is fairly standard. Suppose, for example, that the sample of innovations used, I_1, is a
subset of the unobserved total population of innovations, I,
introduced by firm i or in sector j at time t. The measurement
error is $I_2 \equiv I - I_1$. Let the true model of the effects of innovation be

$$Y = \theta I + \varepsilon, \tag{1}$$

where Y is some measure of performance (e.g. industry productivity growth or corporate profitability). If I_1 is used instead
of I in (1), then the unobserved component of the model becomes $(\varepsilon - I_2)$, and, as is well known, estimates of θ will be
biased down, i.e. the effects of innovation will be understated.
Much the same argument applies if one uses only a subset of
innovation inputs, R, to measure innovative output I. Suppose,
for example, that innovations are produced from a kind of
production function of the form

$$I = \alpha R + Z, \tag{2}$$

where R might reflect the number of scientists and engineers
employed in R. & D. labs and Z all other scientists and engineers conversant with the technology who are also employed in
the firm. If R is used rather than I in (1), then the unobserved
component in (1) becomes $(\varepsilon + \theta Z)$, and exactly the same argument suggests that a regression of R on Y will understate the

effects of I on Y. What is worse, θ cannot be identified in such a regression.

The first measurement error problem is created by the possibility that spillovers may loosen the link between a firm's own R. & D. inputs and its output of innovations. Knowledge has many of the characteristics of a public good, and the use of a firm's own R. & D. expenditures as a measure of its innovative activity will understate the possible contribution of rivals and of other firms up and down the value chain whenever rivals cannot fully appropriate the knowledge which they create. If one thinks of Z as capturing these spillovers, then estimates of θ in (1) that use only R as a proxy for I will understate the true value of θ: spillovers from j's R. & D. to i's innovation production process are neglected (as are spillovers from i to j) and, as a consequence, the total productivity of that R. & D. is understated. The most obvious remedy for this problem is to include j's R. & D. in i's performance equation, but, in the absence of direct observations of knowledge-flows, it is hard to be sure that all spillovers are taken account of. This problem may, however, not be as serious as it first looks. If firms must make investments in research to benefit from spillovers, then R and Z are likely to be positively correlated. In this case, estimates of θ may provide a reasonably accurate measure of the sum of both the direct (via I) and the indirect (via the unobserved Z and then I) effects of R on Y. Further, if knowledge is less portable when it is embodied in a specific innovative outputs than when it is first generated by R. & D., then innovation counts (or, perhaps patent counts) are likely to yield more reliable estimates of θ than R. & D. expenditures.

A second problem with measuring the performance effects of an innovation is that the returns to innovations are typically shared in one way or another between innovation producers and innovation users. Further, the degree to which sharing occurs may depend on the structure and conditions of appropriability that exist in this intermediate market (e.g. see von Hippel, 1988). It follows that studies of performance using (1) which focus only on producers or only on users are not only likely to understate the total benefits of innovation, but they may also yield biased estimates of the return to one or other party if the division of the spoils is affected by those factors which create errors in measuring I, by factors which are summarized in Z or by other variables (like firm size or market structure) which are included in (1) to correct for *ceteris paribus* conditions. In a sense, this problem is similar to that created by spillovers (both arise from problems of less than complete appropriability): a failure to track down all of the value created by an innovation for all agents in the economy may lead one to understate the total benefits of that innovation.

A third type of measurement error arises when patent statistics and innovation counts omit unsuccessful innovations (as they typically do). Omitting unsuccessful innovations by using data only on successful innovations in (1) is likely to lead to an overstatement of the returns to investing in innovative activity (i.e. estimates of θ in (1) may be biased up), not least because firms often learn from failed innovations, and this learning is likely to be reflected in their performance. Estimates of the returns to successful innovations may also be affected by this problem if other variables included as controls in (1) are determinants of the probability that a firm makes a successful innovation. In this context, measures of innovation inputs (like R. & D.) may produce more reliable estimates of the returns to investments in innovative activities than measures of (successful) innovative output.

Measurement error also affects studies of the causes of innovative activity. Suppose the true model of innovative activity is

$$I = \beta X + \mu, \tag{3}$$

where X is, say, a measure of firm size or market structure. The use of I_1 or R rather than I on the left-hand side of (3) adds a term to the residual proportional to I_2 or Z respectively. The size and direction of bias in this case depends on the relationship between X and I_2 or Z. As we noted above, if X has a similar effect on both I_1 and I_2, then estimates of β derived from a regression of X on I_1 may more accurately measure the effect that X has on I than it measures the effect that X has on I_1. If, by contrast, X increases I_1 only because it decreases I_2, then estimates of β will understate the effects of X on I_1 and will not provide accurate information on the effects of X on total innovative activity, I.

The fourth measurement error problem is that of fully correcting for variations in 'technological opportunity'. Different technologies are more or less fecund, and the marginal productivity of any given research input may depend on a wide array of factors which are impossible to measure. Thinking of these factors as captured by Z, then a failure to include Z in a regression of R on Y will clearly lead to bias. More worrying, if Z is

correlated to X, say because industries which are rich in technological opportunities are also highly concentrated, then this
measurement error is likely to erroneously inflate estimates of
β in models of the determinants of innovation like (3). It is not
hard to believe that a correlation between Z and market structure will exist if previous innovations have had a big effect on
current market structure or if conditions of 'technological opportunity' affect entry barriers, and this means that erroneous
inferences about the role played by firm size or market structure may result from incomplete corrections for variations in
'technological opportunity'.

The fifth measurement error is that the choice of different
proxies for I may lead to the estimation of a spurious positive
correlation between firm size and innovation. In particular,
R. & D. activities are typically undertaken by large firms, and
there is some evidence to suggest that the R. & D. activities of
small firms are underreported in most official statistics despite
the fact that their contribution to total innovative output can
be considerable (see Kleinknecht, 1987; Cohen and Klepper,
1992, examine the intra-industry distribution of R. & D. activity). Further, small firms seem to have a lower propensity to
patent than large firms, not least because the fixed costs of
patent registration and protection are likely to weigh more
heavily on firms with a smaller revenue base. Finally, since the
activities of large firms are often easier to observe than smaller
firms, studies of innovation counts are somewhat more likely
to include their innovations than those of their smaller rivals.
The first argument suggests that R. & D. statistics will be positively correlated with firm size almost by construction, while
the second two arguments suggest that patent or innovation
counts may be positively correlated to firm size by construction
unless some care is taken in assembling the data. It follows
that most studies of the relationship between firm size and
innovation are, by construction, likely to generate a positive
correlation between innovation and firm size even if the true
relationship is negative or non-existent. Since it is almost impossible to correct the underreporting of R. & D. by smaller
firms, one is more likely to observe a positive correlation between R. & D. and firm size than between patents or innovation counts and firm size, and this is in fact what one observes
(e.g. see Geroski and Stewart, 1991).

The bottom line, then, is that innovation counts, although not
perfect, are (arguably) the most reliable indicator of innovative

activity which one can use in exploring the link between innovation, market structure, and corporate performance. At the
very least, they have the great virtue of measuring the phenomena that firms who invest in R. & D. are trying to produce, and
that firms who take out patents are trying to protect. Further,
it is innovative output which directly impacts on markets, not
R. & D. or patents. If they are carefully constructed, innovation
counts may avoid the clear sample construction bias which is
evident in many R. & D. data-sets, and they may suffer less
from problems associated with a failure to completely measure
spillovers. Further, if the innovations count data are drawn
from a reasonably well-defined population, then it will suffer
from a less severe 'apples and oranges' problem than patent
counts. Even still, the use of innovations data is likely to lead
to an understatement of the consequences of innovative activity when innovation producers do not use their own innovations, and to an overstatement of the returns to innovation
when unsuccessful innovations are not included in the data.
Further, the uncritical use of innovations data may lead to a
spurious link between innovative activity on the one hand and
firm size or market structure on the other if corrections for
'technological opportunity' are incomplete or if the data have
been badly constructed.

3. *The SPRU Innovations Database*

The data that we will be using in this book are drawn from a
large survey of innovative activity undertaken by the Science
Policy Research Unit (SPRU) at the University of Sussex. The
data consist of 4,378 'major' innovations produced in the UK
over the period 1945–83. The survey was motivated by a desire
to collect useful data on indicators of scientific and technological advantage '*to provide more systematic statistical information
on the sources, nature and impact of significant innovations in
the UK since 1945*' (Townsend *et al.*, 1981: 21). The SPRU re-
searchers chose to concentrate on 'significant' and not 'incremental' technological innovations, and did not try to study the
social, managerial, and political innovations that accompanied
these technological innovations. They also did not try to include invention or diffusion in the study, although they did
collect information on the first use of the innovations included
in their sample.

The two criteria that were used to determine which innovations to include in the data were: first, that they involve '*the successful commercial introduction of new product or process*' (p. 21); and, second, that it be certified by a body of experts to be a '*significant*' technical advance. In total, SPRU contacted about 400 experts (roughly five or six per sector) from research institutes, trade associations, universities, firms, and the government to list the major innovations which were produced during the time-period in their sector of expertise. Most of the innovations which made it on to the final sample were confirmed by more than one expert. A pilot study was run on two sectors to test the consistency of the information received between different experts with the same sectoral expertise, and this suggested that conflicts between experts might not be a severe problem (see Townsend *et al.*, 1981: 33–8). In particular, the suggestions made by a first group of experts were shown to a second group of experts with the same sectoral expertise, and the percentage of innovations thought significant by the first group but not by the second was 2 per cent in Coal-Mining Machinery and 12.3 per cent in Electronic Components (which fell to 5.4 per cent when one outlying expert's suggestions were discarded).

Three features of the data-collection process which may have a profound effect on the properties of the data are worth noting: the efforts made to include small firms, the times-series consistency of the data, and the comparability between sectors. Consider each in turn.

The SPRU team was particularly alert to potential large-firm biases, and part of their motivation in undertaking a wide consultative exercise as part of their sample construction was to overcome this problem. Since only 30 per cent of their experts were located in private-sector firms, it is reasonable to believe (but hard to prove) that they have been reasonably successful in this respect. As we shall see in a moment, large firms are not the major source of innovations in these data, and in this sense they have been successful. That many small firms have been responsible for the major innovations recorded in the sample does not, however, mean that their sample accurately reflects the size distribution of innovating firms.

The second potentially troubling feature of the data-collection process is the fact that the data were collected in three waves. A first survey was done for the period 1945–70 and identified 1,304 innovations, a second for the period 1970–80 added 848

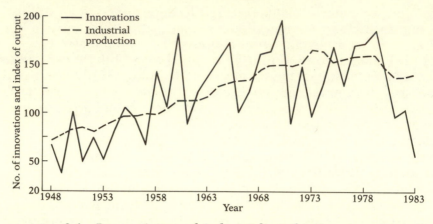

FIG. 2.1   Innovations and industrial production over time

innovations, and a third covered the period 1945–80 and then extended the data to 1983, netting a further 2,226 innovations. Fig. 2.1 shows the variation in the total number of innovations counted by SPRU over time. Two features of the data stand out. First, the annual fluctuations in innovative activity are large, and it is possible to discern some high-frequency clustering of innovations into three- or four-year bursts observable in the late 1950s, the middle 1960s, the late 1960s, and the late 1970s. Although it is not difficult to believe that innovative activity occurs in clusters, fluctuations in the year-by-year totals may reflect any inaccuracies in dating if experts use focal-point dates (e.g. 1960, 1965, 1970, . . .) when they are unsure of precise dates. Second, although there is a general upward trend in the number of innovations produced in the UK over the period, the number of innovations produced in the early 1980s plummeted. Although it is possible this fall-off occurred because of the unusually severe recession which beached the UK manufacturing sector during that period, one cannot avoid the suspicion that at least some of the fall-off is an artefact of the sample collection procedure. In particular, the ending points of the first two waves of data collection (1970 and 1980) were covered at least twice by the SPRU research team, and show no obvious or major fall-off in innovation counts. However, the post-1980 period was covered only once, and only then at the tail-end of what was a long and exhausting study. Further, to the extent that hindsight is an important part of the process of appreciating what is and is not a 'significant' innovation, the innovation counts for the final three or four years of the sample may also understate the total amount of innovative activity that occurred after 1980.

Although it is something of a digression, it is worth noting that Fig. 2.1 also suggests that the innovative activity covered by the data is broadly pro-cyclical. The general upward drift in innovation counts over time is matched by a general upward drift in industrial production, and both series turn down in the early 1980s. A more detailed analysis by Geroski and Walters (1993) suggests that there is a causal relation running from variations in industrial production to variations in innovative activity, but not from innovation to industrial production. Further, although the two series are non-stationary, it is possible to detect signs that the two variables are co-integrated, meaning that there appears to be something that looks like a stable long-run equilibrium relationship between the two. Estimates of that relationship suggest that the elasticity of innovation with respect to output is about 2.0, indicating that innovative activity fluctuates more over the cycle than production does (*ceteris paribus*). Since the innovations in these data are dated from the time of their commercial introduction, these results are probably best interpreted as suggesting that the implementation (but possibly not the invention) of new products and processes is sensitive to demand conditions.

Finally, a potentially troubling feature of the SPRU data-collection process is the question of how comparable the data are across sectors; that is, whether the implicit criteria of 'significant' is comparable across sectors. Table 2.1 displays the main interindustry differences in innovation counts revealed by the data. The first column displays the number of innovations produced in each of nineteen sectors. The three Engineering sectors accounted for nearly 60 per cent of the innovations recorded in the sample; Chemicals is the fourth largest producer, accounting for just over 9 per cent of the total. The SPRU team compared these totals to information on R. & D. expenditures and patenting activity in the UK and to patenting activity in the USA, concluding that Aerospace was 'grossly' underrepresented in the data, Chemicals was 'somewhat' underrepresented, and Metal, Instruments, and Textiles were overrepresented (e.g. see Robson *et al.*, 1988). They also noted an increase in the importance of Textile Machinery and Instruments over time as producers of innovations between the first and second survey, and argued that it '*probably reflects changes*

Table 2.1. Innovative activity by industrial sector

Sector	No. of innovations produced	% innovations produced that are used in other sectors	No. of innovations used
Agriculture	15	16.7	121
Mining	18	47.6	279
Food	82	50.9	105
Chemicals	413	80.8	167
Metals	189	43.0	190
Mech. Eng.	1,241	77.0	408
Instruments	546	80.2	120
Elec. Eng.	793	60.2	383
Shipbuilding	137	49.3	112
Vehicles	226	40.6	263
Aerospace	141	37.6	175
Textiles	146	16.7	481
Bricks, etc.	148	59.2	105
Paper	40	53.7	65
Printing	15	20.7	104
Rubber, Plastics	122	63.5	57
Construction	43	46.2	189
Utilities	24	41.5	240
Services	38	59.5	813

Sources: Adapted from Robson *et al.* (1988: Table 2) and Pavitt *et al.* (1989: Table 2).

in our data collection procedure and levels of response from experts' (Townsend *et al.*, 1981: 32). Other changes in innovative activity which seemed to be unrelated to the data-collection procedure were the increased importance of Electronics and a decline in the importance of Chemicals and Steel as innovation producers (Robson *et al.*, 1988: 10).

Of these apparent intersectoral anomalies, it is the seeming underrepresentation of Aerospace which is the most troubling. The concern arises because Aerospace is a very heavy R. & D. spender (its share of R. & D. expenditures in 1967 was about 28 per cent) but a low innovator (it accounts for about 1.5 per cent of the sample of innovations). It is hard to be sure whether this apparent lack of innovativeness is due to the use of commercial criteria in the selection procedure (Aerospace produces mainly defence-related innovations), or whether it reflects an unusually high ratio of R. & D. expenditures per innovation in this sector. It is certainly true that Aerospace is a relatively low-patenting sector, and its ranking by patenting activity is not out of line with its ranking by innovation counts. Similarly but perhaps less troubling, Instruments is a very high innovator (accounting for about 12.5 per cent of the total innovations in the data) but does very little R. & D. (accounting for about 2.3 per cent of total R. & D. in 1967). Its ranking by patenting activities is, however, similar to its innovation-count ranking. Chemicals, by contrast, is a much heavier patenter than it is an R. & D. spender or innovator (see Townsend *et al.*, 1983: Table 4.3).

These apparent anomalies led the SPRU experts to put somewhat more faith in the consistency of their experts' views over time than they did in the differences between the views of experts in different sectors. Although it would be foolhardy to ignore the views of those who collected the data, it seems to me that these apparent anomalies in ranking the innovativeness of different sectors may also spring from a rather strong reliance on the use of R. & D. expenditures to measure innovativeness. I am, therefore, somewhat less concerned about biases in the measurement of intersectoral differences in innovativeness than they seem to be. Further, it is hard to believe that the heavy dominance of the Engineering sector as an innovation producer is an artefact of the construction of the data, and it is innovations produced in Engineering which underlie two of the most interesting and unexpected features of the data.

4. *Users and Producers, Small and Large Firms*

There are two properties of the SPRU innovations data which are both interesting in their own right, and important to understand for what follows. First, very few of the innovations in the data were first used by the firm that produced them, and, indeed, few were first used in the same sector as they were produced. Second, small firms produced a large share of these innovations. Consider each in turn.

Users and producers

The first column on Table 2.1 shows the number of innovations produced in each of nineteen sectors (allocated by identifying the principal activity of the innovation-producing unit), the second column shows the percentage of these which were first used in other sectors (allocated by identifying the principal activity of the innovation-using firm), and the third shows the number of innovations used in each sector. As we noted earlier, the big innovation producers are the three Engineering sectors and Chemicals, who collectively accounted for about 68 per cent of the innovations in the sample. By contrast, the big users are Services, Textiles, Mechanical Engineering, and Mining, who collectively used about 45 per cent of the innovations in the sample. Of these four big users, only Mechanical Engineering is also a big producer of innovations, and, even then, most of the innovations used in Mechanical Engineering were produced in another sector. Only 120 innovations (or about 3 per cent of the total) were produced in the four non-manufacturing sectors shown on the table, but these sectors used 1,363 innovations (or about 31 per cent of the total).

The fact that nearly 70 per cent of the innovations in the sample were not first used in the sector which produced them and that Engineering is a particularly heavy producer and exporter of innovations is not a surprise. Any selection criteria which emphasizes commercial success as an indicator of whether an innovation is 'major' is bound to generate a sample in which the ratio of 'process' (i.e. own use) to 'product' (i.e. others use) innovations is very low. Since new innovations often need to be embodied in, or accompanied by, specific types of capital equipment, Engineering is bound to be both a major producer and a major exporter of innovations. It is, however, interesting to speculate on what other factors might underlie the apparently wide diffusion of the innovations in these data. It has long been appreciated that a successful innovation must couple user needs with producers' skills, and, indeed, that users may play a major role in the design of new innovations. Further, the evidence compiled by von Hippel (1988) suggests that users play a major role in the innovation process in the Scientific Instruments sector, and it is not hard to believe that a similar relationship between users and producers exists elsewhere in Engineering (not least because many Engineering firms are rather small). If it is indeed the case that many of the innovations produced in Engineering are user driven, then one expects to see many of the gains to Engineering innovations accruing to users.

Fig. 2.2 maps out the major flows of innovations throughout the economy. At the core of this network are the three Engineering sectors, and it is evident that there is a major flow of

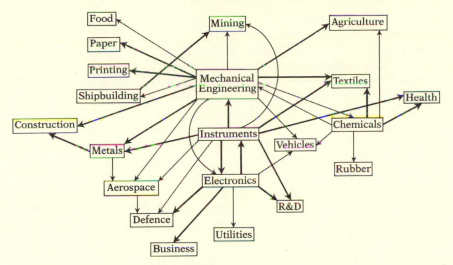

FIG. 2.2   The intersectoral flow of innovations

innovations within this group, particularly between Instruments and Electronics. Textiles, Mining, and Electronics are major users of Mechanical Engineering innovations (accounting for about 42 per cent of the total produced), Textiles, R. & D., and Health are major users of Instruments (accounting for 28 per cent of the total), and Defence, Business, and R. & D. are major users of Electronics innovations (accounting for 26 per cent of the total). Just under 40 per cent of the Electronics innovations are 'process' innovations, much higher than the 23 per cent and 20 per cent of 'process' innovations recorded by Mechanical Engineering and Instruments respectively. Unsurprisingly, the other big innovations producer, Chemicals, forms its own distinct hub, exporting 80 per cent of its innovations mainly to Health, Textiles, and Agriculture. Fig. 2.2 also suggests that an alternative way of organizing the data is to focus on core-using sectors. Textiles, Health, Instruments, and Electronics stand out as core users not only because they are major importers of innovations produced elsewhere, but also because they appear to be focal points for the activities of more than one of the major producing sectors.

Modern growth theory has begun to explore models in which economic growth is driven endogenously by the growth of knowledge (e.g. see Grossman and Helpman, 1991). Since knowledge is a public good, growth is, in part, driven in these models by externalities and increasing returns to the application of knowledge. This kind of theorizing tempts one to try to construct a mental map of the economy whose most prominent feature is a collection of 'strategic sectors' defined by the importance of the knowledge which they produce, and the abundance of externalities which they generate. However, to use Fig. 2.2 in this way, one must be clear about just exactly what innovation counts do and do not measure. The fact that the Engineering sector exports numerous innovations does not necessarily mean that it generates numerous externalities: that so much information is embodied in the products produced in this sector may mean that little information spills out from this sector through other means. Further, the fact that this sector produces so many innovations does not necessarily mean that it produces a lot of new knowledge, for many of the most important information inputs may come from users. Indeed, the fact that Engineering produces so many innovations does not mean that 'Engineering matters', since it is more than evident from Fig. 2.2 that Engineering would produce far fewer innovations if many of its major using sectors disappeared. Still, all of this said, one cannot avoid the feeling that there are important focal points in the network of innovative activity which flows between sectors. Of these, Engineering (followed at some distance by Chemicals) stands out as both a major producer and a major user of innovations, and Manufacturing as a whole is an important exporter to non-Manufacturing.

Small and large firms

The second interesting feature of the data is that small firms are important producers of innovations. The SPRU team collected three employment-based measures of firm size (the size of the innovating unit, the UK size of the firm owning that unit, and the world size of the firm owning the innovating unit), and all three show a similar pattern of association between the production of innovations and firm size. Table 2.2 summarizes some of the salient features of the data. The first two columns show the ratio of innovation share to employment share (by UK size of firm) for ten size-classes of firms, while the third, fourth, and fifth columns of Table 2.2 show the percentage of innovations produced by firms ranked according to the three definitions of size. The final column shows some data on R. & D. expenditures by size of firm.

Table 2.2. Innovative activity by firm size

	Ratio of innovation share to employment share		Percent of innovations, 1945–83 by employment size			R. & D. exp. 1975
	1956–60	1976–80	Innovating unit	UK size	World	
1–99	.28	.63	22.8	17	14.5	
100–199	.66	2.07				18.6
200–499	.80	1.58	26.1	16.6	12.6	21.8
500–999	1.04	.92				
1,000–1,999	1.07	.34	37.8	24.4	19	90.4
2,000–4,999	.81	.91				
5,000–9,999	.91	.37				107.3
10,000–19,999	1.68	1.07	11.1	22.6	25.2	
20,000–49,999	1.25	1.05				971.8
50,000+	2.46	1.90	2.2	19.3	28.7	

Source: Adapted from Pavitt *et al.* (1987: Tables II, IV, and V).

Three features of the data stand out in Table 2.2. First, the relative innovation share of small firms (less than 500 employees) rose markedly over the period, being much higher at the end of the period than at the beginning. Only very small and very large firms have a higher innovation share than employment share, and by the end of the period, firms in the size class 100–500 UK employees were significantly outperforming even very large firms (10,000-plus employees). Second, while large global corporations with UK employment above 10,000 employees accounted for nearly 42 per cent of all innovations, nearly 34 per cent of all innovations were produced in relatively small innovating units (less than 1,000 UK employees). Third and finally, while very large firms (in excess of 10,000 UK employees) accounted for more than 80 per cent of all R. & D. expenditures in 1973, their share of innovations produced over the period was half this size. By contrast, small UK firms (less than 500 employees) accounted for only 1.5 per cent of total R. & D. expenditures in 1973, much much less than their share of innovations produced.

These data create a number of difficulties for those who believe that large firm-size and technological progressiveness go hand in hand. It seems clear that large firms do undertake most of the R. & D. done in the UK economy, but they do not account for the lion's share of innovative output. Indeed, the ratio of innovations produced to R. & D. expenditures is clearly and very strongly negatively correlated with firm size, however measured. Further, innovations are generally produced in innovation units of only very modest size, and, in fact, there is a mildly negative association between the size of innovation units and the number of innovations which they produce. Finally, the relation between innovations produced and firm size is, if anything, U-shaped: just over 75 per cent of all innovations are produced by firms whose UK employment is either below 1,000 employees or above 10,000 employees. What makes the data difficult to interpret, however, is the possibility that small innovating units and small innovating firms may produce innovations with the support of large users (or, indeed, that many apparently independent innovating units are actually part of larger organizations; see Smith *et al.*, 1993: 60). Indeed, the footloose nature of most of these innovations makes one wonder whether the relationship between innovation and user size (which we unfortunately have no information on) might be more interesting to examine than that between innovation and producer size.

The importance of small firms in the innovation process varies across sectors in a number of interesting ways, and Table 2.3 shows the number of innovations produced by firms in five size-classes across nineteen sectors. Even a quick glance at the data reveals that the three Engineering sectors are responsible for much of the innovative output of small firms. Of the 640 innovations produced by firms whose UK employment is less than 200 employees, 419 (or 65 per cent) were produced in these three sectors. Similarly, these three sectors account for 328 of the 557 innovations (or 59 per cent) produced by firms whose employment fell between 200 and 1,000 employees. Small firms are also important producers of innovations in Services, Textiles, and Printing. By contrast, 329 out of the 421 innovations (or 78 per cent) produced in Chemicals were produced by firms whose UK employment exceeded 10,000. Large firms were also the dominant producers of innovations in Mining, Food, Vehicles, Metals, Aerospace, and Utilities.

These results will come as a surprise only to those whose view of the innovation process starts and ends with R. & D. expenditures. There is no doubt that formalized R. & D. activity has become a regular feature of the bundle of activities that many large firms undertake (for an historical account of the development of this phenomena, see Mowery and Rosenberg, 1989). Those who think about innovation activities in terms of R. & D. decisions are frequently willing to allow R. & D. spillovers from rivals into their models as an additional input, but they rarely give much attention to non-R. & D. inputs and they almost never pay much attention to the role of users or suppliers in the innovation process. The SPRU innovations data encourage one to think much more broadly (and speculatively) about the determinants of innovative output, and to concentrate much more on the contributions to innovation made by firms operating throughout the value chain. It seems clear that the absence of formalized R. & D. activity presents no obstacles for firms interested in producing major innovations, and one cannot entirely escape the feeling that flows of information between producers and users may be more important than those between rivals. Needless to say, in this rather broader vision of the innovation process, the question of whether large firms are more technologically progressive than small ones seems

Table 2.3. Number of innovations produced by firms of different size across sectors

Sector	1968 SIC classification	1–199 employees	200–999 employees	1,000–9,999 employees	10,000–49,000 employees	50,000+ employees
Agriculture	001–3	1	0	8	3	0
Mining	101–4	0	3	1	16	106
Food	211–40	4	6	11	64	27
Chemicals	261–79	20	31	41	132	197
Metals	311–23	1	7	48	28	102
Mech. Eng.	331–49	228	222	296	285	100
Instruments	351–4	105	60	51	55	61
Elec. Eng.	361–9	86	46	67	170	405
Shipbuilding	370	9	10	31	16	1
Vehicles	380–2,384–5	20	18	61	58	55
Aerospace	383	2	6	15	25	37
Textiles	411–50	29	17	47	10	41
Bricks etc.	461–9	22	12	29	76	18
Paper	481–4	9	11	7	21	6
Printing	485–9	2	10	16	1	0
Rubber, Plastics	471–9,491–9	14	25	1	14	37
Construction	500	12	3	13	10	1
Utilities	601–3,701–9	3	3	9	14	53
Services	810–99	73	67	32	65	87

Source: Adapted from Pavitt et al. (1987: Table VI).

somewhat less pressing than it does when one concentrates only on R. & D. decisions.

5. Conclusions

Our goal in what follows is to identify the major features of the relationship between innovation, market structure, and corporate performance. Our methodology will be statistical, and we shall use a consistent body of data on the number of 'major' innovations produced and used in the UK over the post-war period. As with all databases, this sample has a number of limitations, and its use is likely to create a number of biases. Although the use of data on successful innovations runs the risk of exaggerating the rate of return to innovative activity, our expectation is that the fact that most of the innovations were not used by the firms which produced them means that the real risk we run is that of understating the returns to innovation. The data provide information only on the first use of these innovations and do not identify using firms (they do, however, identify using sectors), and this will inevitably focus our work on innovation producers. Although the existence of spillovers may create problems, it is the lack of good information on users' performance which, we conjecture, will give rise to the substantive problems. On the other hand, these data do have the great virtue of focusing attention on that part of the innovative process which directly affects market processes, and they seem to be relatively free of firm-size biases. Provided that we are able to successfully correct for variations in 'technological opportunity', it seems reasonable to believe that the data may provide a reasonably accurate assessment of the determinants of innovative activity.

3 Innovation and the Evolution of Market Structure*

1. *Introduction*

While it is easy to believe that technology has an important influence on market structure, it is less certain that the post-war rise in market concentration observed in many advanced economies is largely a consequence of the introduction of new centralizing technological innovations. This doubt arises partly because it is possible to believe that increased product differentiation, rising pecuniary advantages of firm size, or purely stochastic effects may be the real culprit, and partly because of a rather interesting hypothesis due to Blair (1972). Blair argued that, from the middle or late eighteenth century until early in the present one, technological change effectively increased the minimum efficient scale of most manufacturing plants, and raised the capital outlays required to build them. However, the relatively recent introduction of new materials such as plastics, new power-creating technologies such as high-energy batteries, and the increasing use of computers and multipurpose machines were seen by him as being fundamentally decentralizing. If it is true that such twentieth-century innovations have reduced minimum efficient scale, then it is difficult to accept the view that recent increases in market concentration follow from some relentless and unyielding technological imperative. In this chapter, we provide some evidence

* With Richard Pomroy; first published in, and reprinted with the permission of, the *Journal of Industrial Economics*, 38 (1990): 299–314. We are obliged to seminar participants at Southampton, the IIM in Berlin, the 1988 EARIE Meeting in Rotterdam, and the ESRC Industrial Economics Study Group meeting held at the LBS, January 1988, for useful discussions of this research. Some of the data used here were obtained from the ESRC Data Archive at the University of Essex, and the research was supported by the ESRC. Mark Casson, Geoff Stewart, Dick Allard, Steve Davies, Bo Carlsson, and two referees provided comments, and Jim Fairburn assisted with the data-collection and also provided helpful comments throughout. At the end of the day, however, the usual disclaimer applies.

on the evolution of market structure which is consistent with the Blair hypothesis. In particular, our data suggest that the major innovations introduced in a wide range of industries in the UK during the 1970s were decentralizing, and lowered levels of market concentration (*ceteris paribus*).

The method that Blair used to examine his hypothesis focused on a small number of specific innovations, examining each in some detail, and then speculating on the wider implications of each for manufacturing operations in general. Without wishing to suggest that it is anything other than complementary, our method concentrates on charting the effect of a wide range of innovations on market concentration across a wide range of industries using familiar cross-section regression techniques. We proceed in three stages. The main problem to be faced in examining the effect of innovation on market structure is to separate short- from long-run changes in the observed movements in market concentration. This is a familiar problem, and Section 2 outlines a not unfamiliar solution to it. The results of applying this model to two 73-industry cross-section panels for the UK covering the 1970s are presented in Section 3. Amongst several other things, they suggest that actual market structure adjusts rather rapidly to changes in long-run concentration levels, a finding in sharp conflict with much of the empirical literature on this subject. Our conclusions, presented in Section 4, trace the interaction between the role of market structure in the process generating new innovations and the effect of innovation on market structure. Here our results point to a quick-acting and mutually reinforcing cycle which is, however, of only modest strength. Put crudely, competition stimulates innovation and innovation increases the degree of competition in markets, both effects leading in principle to a steady rise in the rate of innovation and to a steady fall in market concentration over time.

2. Modelling the Dynamics of Market Structure

To examine the association between innovation and changes in long-run levels of concentration, it is necessary to decompose observed changes on concentration into changes arising from short-run disequilibrium dynamics, changes due to shifts in long-run equilibrium, and purely transitory changes. The common procedure followed in this type of situation is to posit the existence of some kind of costs of adjustment which cause agents to dampen and delay their responses to new events[1]. Lags in adjustment by agents imply that there will only be a partial adjustment of actual to long-run equilibrium levels of concentration in any given period, and thus that current-period changes in concentration will be a fraction of the last period's deviation from equilibrium. If the long-run level of concentration does not change over time, then this kind of rule leads to a zero steady-state error, and thus is not an unreasonable one to expect agents to follow (e.g. see Salmon, 1982). However, were long-run concentration levels to grow or decline steadily, then this type of partial adjustment rule would never bring actual concentration levels into equality with long-run levels. In these circumstances, it is reasonable to suppose that agents will incorporate anticipated changes in the target into their adjustment rule, since this will ensure convergence at least in the steady state. The result is that current period changes in concentration will depend not only on last period's deviation from equilibrium, but also on current (and possibly expected future) changes in the equilibrium level of concentration.

This argument suggests that an appropriate model of the evolution of market structure over time might be

$$\Delta C_t = \gamma_0 [C^*_t - C_{t-1}] + \gamma_1 \Delta C^*_t, \qquad (1)$$

where C_t is the actual level of market concentration, C_t^* is the long-run equilibrium level of concentration, and Δ is the first difference operator.[2] In words, (1) states that observed changes in concentration are the sum of changes induced by disequilibrium and changes due to shifts in long-run equilibrium configurations, with weights γ_0 and γ_1 depending on the relative

---

[1] The most well-known type of adjustment cost is that described by the so-called 'Penrose effect'; see Penrose (1959) and Slater (1980). Lags may also arise because of delays from suppliers of equipment for new plants, obstacles to the perception of new opportunities, and so on.

[2] This type of error-correction formulation of dynamics was first introduced by Davidson *et al.* (1978) and Davidson and Hendry (1981); Nickell (1985) contains an excellent exposition of the basic ideas involved. Briefly, this formulation emerges if one assumes that the process of competition can be mimicked by a mechanism which adjusts actual concentration levels, C_t, to desired levels, C_t^*, in a manner which minimizes a loss function,

$$L = (\lambda_1/2)(\Delta C_t)^2 + (\lambda_2/2)(C_t - C_t^*)^2 - \lambda_3(\Delta C_t)(\Delta C_t^*),$$

where $\lambda_1, \lambda_2, \lambda_3 > 0$. The first term captures adjustment costs arising from changing market shares, the second captures costs of being out of equilibrium, and the third penalizes adjustment in the 'wrong' direction. Minimizing L by choice of C_t yields (1), where $\gamma_0 \equiv \lambda_2/(\lambda_1 + \lambda_2)$ and $\gamma_1 \equiv \lambda_3/(\lambda_1 + \lambda_2)$.

size of various costs of adjustment. In the empirical work that follows, only γ_0 is identified. $\gamma_0 = 0$ if the costs of being out of equilibrium are dominated by the costs of adjusting to changes in the long-run equilibrium position, while $\gamma_0 = 1$ if costs of adjustment are relatively small. Adding a residual, ε_t, to (1) completes the decomposition of observed changes in market concentration into changes due to short-run disequilibrium dynamics, changes due to shifts in long-run equilibrium, and purely transitory changes.[3]

That equation (1) is a fairly standard applied econometric representation of market-structure dynamics is not, of course, sufficient to make it a compelling one. We interpret C_t^* as the level of concentration that would be generated as an equilibrium of an oligopoly game; that is, it is a function of the rules of the game plus the full range of relevant exogenous variables (for an example, see Vickers, 1986). It reflects the *long-run equilibrium* implicit in the data—it is what would be observed at t were it the case that all the effects of changes in the exogenous variables at t had manifested themselves in t. On the face of it, this is an unlikely outcome, and what we observe, C_t, is interpreted as *temporary equilibrium* that results from only those effects which are actually registered in t. Given these definitions, it is clear that C and C^* can differ because there are costs to responding to shifts in exogenous variables, costs that may exceed the costs of being out of long-run equilibrium. The major virtue of (1) is that it enables one to determine whether C_t does equal C_t^* in any period t, and, if not, it enables one to compute the effects that various exogenous variables of interest have on market structure in both types of equilibrium. Its major shortcoming is that it restricts the ratio of short- and long-run effects to be the same for each exogenous variable. This restriction can be alleviated slightly by allowing (as we shall do) the exogenous variables to have effects on ΔC_t^* that differ from those that they have on C_t^*. The model also effectively assumes that the exogenous variables affect only long-run equilibria and not the speed of adjustment towards them. This is, in some sense, a matter of choosing how to interpret the data. Since

[3] The major conceptual limitation of (1) is that agents do not anticipate future movements in C_t^*, and this arises from the static nature of the minimization problem discussed in n. 2. The model can easily be generalized to allow for an infinitely long planning horizon, an extension which has only a minor effect on the empirical model and, as it turns out, no substantive effects on the empirical results. Details of the extended model can be obtained from the authors on request.

neither long-run equilibria nor speeds of adjustment are directly observable, partitioning the effects of changes in the exogenous variables between the two will always be slightly arbitrary. One might see an exogenous variable like innovation affecting adjustment costs or, following the habit of most economists, as affecting long-run equilibria configurations, but this is not a choice that is amenable to testing.

One further virtue of equation (1) is that it nests most of the models of market structure which have been used in the literature (for a survey, see Curry and George, 1983). Some models have assumed $\gamma_0 = 1$ and $\Delta C^*_t = 0$. With no costs of adjustment and no movement in targets, there is no question of being out of equilibrium, and $C_t = C^*_t$. In practice, this type of model usually involves regressing C_t on various determinants of C^*_t (e.g. Ornstein *et al.*, 1973, Sawyer, 1971, and others). More sophisticated and apparently more consistent with the data are models in which γ_0 is not restricted to equal unity, but these models typically assume that $\Delta C^*_t = 0$. The result is myopic adjustment of the form $\Delta C_t = \gamma_0[C^*_t - C_{t-1}]$. In practice, this type of model usually involves regressing C_t or ΔC_t on various determinants of C^*_t and on C_{t-1} (e.g. Caves and Porter, 1980, Levy, 1985, Geroski *et al.*, 1987, and others). If, in fact, $\Delta C^*_t \neq 0$ and agents respond to such changes when making their decisions at t, then this type of model will generate a systematic error if it is imposed on the data. The result will be biased estimates of γ_0 and of the determinants of C^*_t. For this reason, it seems desirable to start with a model like (1), and then to simplify it in a manner consistent with the data.

The difficulty that all empirical models of concentration have is that C^*_t is not directly observable, and the usual procedure that is followed is to model it as a linear function of various observables. Our major interest is in the effect of technology, τ_t, on market structure. This effect is usually captured by including a proxy for minimum-efficient scale, a practice made dubious by the almost tautological relationship that exists between many of these proxies and measures of concentration (e.g. Davies, 1980). The alternative approach that we are going to explore here springs from the observation that it is far easier to observe changes in technology, $\Delta\tau_t$, than it is to observe or to measure the 'level of technology', τ_t, itself. Current best-practice production techniques are the result of an appropriately depreciated accretion of technical advance over many years, with recent advances having more effect on current best-practice techniques than more distant advances. Hence, rather than trying to measure τ_t directly, one might build up an index of τ_t by examining the history of technical innovation, and we express this as

$$\tau_t = \theta(L)\Delta\tau_t + \mu \approx \theta_0\Delta\tau_t + \theta_1\Delta\tau_{t-1} + \mu, \tag{2}$$

where $\theta(L)$ is a polynomial in the distributed lag operator L, and μ is a fixed industry-specific effect which reflects an inherent or base stock of knowledge to which the $\Delta\tau_t$ are increments. Simplifying $\theta(L)$ to its first two terms reflects an inability to estimate a fuller set of distributed lags with our data.[4]

Of course, other factors affect C^*_t besides τ_t, and some of these are systematic and observable (denoted X_t), while others are not. The observables X_t affect ΔC_t via their effect on C^*_t and via the effect that changes in X_t, ΔX_t, have on ΔC^*_t. In the spirit of putting as few unnecessary restrictions on the empirical model as possible, we shall allow the effect of X_t on C^*_t to differ from that of ΔX_t on ΔC^*_t, in essence because changes in X_t may not be registered immediately on C^*_t. This plus the seemingly natural assumption of linearity yields

$$C^*_t = \beta_0 X_t + \partial\tau_t, \tag{3}$$

and

$$\Delta C^*_t = \beta_1 \Delta X_t + \phi\Delta\tau_t. \tag{4}$$

We take $\Delta\tau_t$ to be observable (it is, by definition, an 'innovation') and use (2) to eliminate the unobservable τ_t in (3), yielding

$$C^*_t = \beta_0 X_t + \delta\theta_0\Delta\tau_t + \delta\theta_1\Delta\tau_{t-1} + \delta\mu. \tag{5}$$

Using (4) and (5), (1) can now be expressed entirely in terms of observables and a residual ε_t,

$$\Delta C_t = \delta\mu + (\gamma_0\beta_0)X_t + (\gamma_1\beta_1)\Delta X_t + (\gamma_0\delta\theta_0 + \phi\gamma_1)\,\Delta\tau_t \\ + (\gamma_0\delta\theta_1)\Delta\tau_{t-1} - \gamma_0 C_{t-1} + \varepsilon_t. \tag{6}$$

In practice, the specification of X_t and ε_t depends partly on what can be observed and partly on what can be omitted without fear of bias. It is common in these models to include measures of market size, Z_t, and, often because it acts as a proxy for technological conditions, capital intensity, K_t. Accepting the risk that it may lead to an understatement of the effect of innovation, we include both and expect them to decrease and to

---

[4] See Griliches and Pakes (1984) for a discussion of the problem of estimating distributed lags using panel data. Prior restrictions on either the shape of $\theta(L)$ or on the process generating $\Delta\tau_{it}$ can be used in the panel context, but we have too few panels to make serious progress on this problem.

increase C^*_t respectively. What is more difficult to measure is the state of product differentiation or various pecuniary advantages to size. Several scholars have included measures of advertising intensity in models of concentration (e.g. Mueller and Rogers, 1980, and others), but these data are not available in the UK for our sample period. At the very least, one can aspire to capturing the important variations in these factors across industries by supposing that they are broadly constant over time, with any departures from constancy being random. This strong but not entirely unappealing assumption enables one to capture such omitted determinants of C^*_t through the fixed effects introduced in equation (2). We thus include industry-specific constants in our specification, and take ε_t to be a zero mean, normally distributed random variable.[5]

In short, we propose to examine the effect of innovations in market structure for a sample of industries, $i = 1, \ldots, N$, in two time-periods, $t = 1, 2$, using the model

$$\Delta C_{it} = f_i + \alpha_1 Z_{it} + \alpha_2 K_{it} + \alpha_3 \Delta Z_{it} + \alpha_4 \Delta K_{it} + \alpha_5 \Delta \tau_{it} + \alpha_6 \Delta \tau_{it-1}$$

$$+ \ \alpha_7 C_{it-1} + \varepsilon_{it}, \tag{7}$$

The two main parameters of interest are $\alpha_5 \equiv \gamma_0 \delta \theta_0 + \phi \gamma_1$ and $\alpha_6 \equiv \gamma_0 \delta \theta_1$. Since θ_0, θ_1, γ_0, and γ_1 are all positive, then α_5 and α_6 will both be negative if the effects of technology on C_t^* and ΔC_t^*, δ and ϕ, are negative. Identifying γ_0 is straightforward and comes directly from α_7.[6] Finally, since γ_1 and γ_0 are non-negative, then α_1 and α_2 have the same sign as the effects of Z_{it} and K_{it} have on C^*_{it}, and similarly with α_3 and α_4.

3. *The Evolution of Market Structure*

Movements in market concentration are, on the whole, rather gradual and, following near-universal practice, we shall model

---

[5] Other determinants of C^*_t that have featured in the literature include measures of multiplant economies (e.g. the plant per firm ratio) and, occasionally, changes in the number of firms (see Curry and George (1983) for further details). Multiplant economies, like minimum efficient scale, reflect the effects of technology on market structure and so are captured in τ_t. Entry seems to be more a mechanism by which changes in market structure occur than a determinant of C^*_t; to the extent that entry depends on the determinants of C^*_t and on the quantity ($C_t - C^*_t$), then its workings are implicit in (1).

[6] If $\beta_0 = \beta_1$ in (3) and (4), then $\alpha_1/\alpha_3 = \alpha_2/\alpha_4 = \gamma_0/\gamma_1$ and yields an overidentifying restriction. In fact, our data suggest that $\beta_0 \neq \beta_1$. This undoubtedly arises from the rather simple structure of (3) and (4), but, since it is difficult to see how this misspecification might lead to biased estimates of α_5, α_6, and α_7, we have not explored it further.

movements in the five-firm concentration ratio over a five-year period. To handle the problem of estimating a full set of industry-specific fixed effects, we use two cross-section panels, 1970–4 and 1975–9.[7] Each cross-section panel includes seventy-three three-digit industries, the sample being weighted towards more technologically progressive industries. The innovations data come from a large survey of 4,378 commercially significant innovations introduced in the UK, 1945–83; $\Delta\tau_{it}$ is simply the number of innovations first used in industry i during the five-year period t. Z_{it} is the log of domestic industry production on average throughout the period, K_{it} is the ratio of capital stock to industry production on average, and ΔZ_{it} and ΔK_{it} are first differences between the beginning and end year of each period. Further details on the data used can be found in the Appendix.

Table 3.1 displays various estimates of equation (7). Multi-collinearity proved to be largely absent in our data, and extensive testing yielded no traces of heteroscedasticity. Predicted values of C_t were extremely close to actual values for regressions (i)–(v) (the correlation was above 0.95 and the means of both series were virtually identical), and no obvious pattern of prediction error was detected. No predictions of C_t fell outside the unit interval. Time-dummies were included in early specifications of (i)–(vi) but were never significant. The results are extremely robust to their exclusion. Restricting attention to regressions (i)–(v), it is clear that the effect of innovations on market concentration is negative. Regression (i) includes both $\Delta\tau_{it}$ and $\Delta\tau_{it-1}$, the coefficient on the former being negative and significant, and that on the latter insignificant. (iv) includes $\Delta\tau_{it-1}$ alone, and it attracts a negative but insignificant coefficient. It seems plain from this that innovations have a more or less instantaneous negative effect on C^*_t. Regression (ii) shows (10) with only $\Delta\tau_{it}$, (iii) shows an instrumental variables estimate allowing $\Delta\tau_{it}$ to be endogenous,[8] and (v) includes a term in $(\Delta\tau_{it})^2$. It seems reasonable to infer from these three regressions that estimates of α_5 which assume that $\Delta\tau_{it}$ is exogenous *may* be biased upwards, and that the effect of $\Delta\tau_{it}$ on C^*_t *may* diminish

[7] We did not transform the data by subtracting means as, with a lagged dependent variable, this would induce bias; see Nickell (1981).

[8] This instrument was generated from a reduced-form OLS regression of $\Delta\tau_{it}$ on a full set of fixed effects, $\Delta\tau_{it-1}$, $(\Delta\tau_{it-1})^2$, the percentages of small firms (i.e. less than 99 employees) in the industry, entry and exit rates, import and export intensity, K_{it}, Z_{it}, ΔK_{it}, and ΔZ_{it}. The innovations equation that helped to specify this reduced form is discussed in Geroski (1987). The fixed effects in this equation capture variations in technological opportunities across sectors, something which a richer data-set might model more explicitly.

Table 3.1. Regressions explaining five-year changes in market concentration

	(i)	(ii)	(iii)	(iv)	(v)	(iv)
Z_t	−.0034	−.0033	−.00084	−.0116	−.0049	−.0045
	(.254)	(.251)	(.0555)	(.840)	(.365)	(.876)
K_t	0.0056	0.0056	0.0058	0.0048	0.0053	0.0013
	(3.64)	(3.67)	(3.66)	(3.03)	(3.24)	(0.365)
ΔZ_t	0.0148	0.0149	0.0176	0.0063	0.0112	0.043
	(0.678)	(0.690)	(0.751)	(0.293)	(0.501)	(1.85)
ΔK_t	0.0035	0.0035	0.0034	0.0035	0.0041	−0.0029
	(1.06)	(1.08)	(1.02)	(1.06)	(1.22)	(0.752)
$\Delta \tau_t$	−0.0011	−0.0011	−0.0014*	—	−0.0020	−0.0026
	(3.87)	(3.59)	(2.03)		(2.56)	(1.27)
$\Delta \tau_{t-1}$	0.00023	—	—	−0.0018	—	—
	(0.145)			(0.969)		
C_{t-1}	−1.082	−1.083	−1.082	−1.078	−1.076	−0.042
	(23.18)	(23.28)	(22.25)	(21.30)	(23.14)	(2.69)
$(\Delta \tau_t)^2$	—	—	—	—	0.6x10⁻⁵	—
					(1.52)	
R^2/SSR	.71/.0545	.71/.0545	.70/.0563	.70/.0570	.71/0540	.067/.3665

* Denotes an instrumental variable (see n. 9).

Notes: Absolute values of t-statistics are given in the brackets below the estimated coefficients. The dependent variable is the change in concentration, 1970–4, 1975–9; C_{t-1} = concentration 1970 and 1975; Z_t = log of domestic production, averaged 1970–4, 1975–9; K_t = capital output ratio, averaged 1970–4, 1975–9; ΔZ_t and ΔK_t are the first differences of Z_t and K_t respectively, defined as Z_t in 1979 less Z_t in 1975, and so on; Δt_t = number of innovations 1970–4, 1975–9; $\Delta \tau_{t-1}$ = number of innovations in 1945–70 divided by 5, 1970–4; $(\Delta \tau_t)^2$ is $\Delta \tau_t$ squared; all equations except (vi) include a full set of fixed effects which are estimated jointly with the unknown coefficients of interest (i.e. the data were not transformed to eliminate the fixed effects). The constant in (vi) = .0393 with a t-statistic = 1.086.

at very high values of $\Delta \tau_{it}$ (i.e. may be closer to zero). It is, in fact, the case that the estimate of $\alpha_5 < 0$ is extremely robust. In addition to the experiments shown in (i)–(v), α_5 was estimated as negative and generally significant when combinations of K_{it}, Z_{it}, and ΔZ_{it} were dropped from (7), as well as when the fixed effects were excluded (see regression (vi)). Taking all of this together, it is difficult to argue that the data are inconsistent with Blair's hypothesis.[9]

[9] Two points about our data ought to be noted when interpreting the results. First, the data refer to first use of innovations, and do not monitor the diffusion in use throughout an industry. Therefore, to the extent that small users adopt faster than large ones, they may understate the total deconcentrating effect of innovation. Second,

Aside from Blair's own work, hints consistent with the results reported here abound in the literature. Using this (Pavitt *et al.*, 1987; see also Chapter 2 above) and other data-sets (e.g. Scherer (1984: ch. 11); Edwards and Gordon (1984) consider major and minor innovations), several scholars have observed that small firms introduce a surprisingly large percentage of major innovations. Acs and Audretsch (1987) suggest that this is particularly true in very innovative, skill-intensive sectors which are in early stages of their life cycles. Although this observation does not strictly imply that the introduction of such innovations will be deconcentrating (because such innovative small firms may not grow relative to market leaders, or, indeed, because in small markets, they may be amongst the leaders), the results shown in Table 3.1 are consistent with the view that, on average, small innovating firms do prosper at the expense of leaders. In much the same spirit, it has been observed that entry rates appear to be positively correlated to innovative activity (e.g. Gort and Kanakayama, 1982, and Geroski, 1991*b*), with both variables rising and falling systematically during the course of industry life cycles (e.g. Gort and Klepper, 1982). Focusing on changes in market concentration and using a regression model similar to our own, Mukhopadhyay (1985) found that concentration fell in high and medium R. & D.-intensive industries in the USA, 1963–77 (but see Farber (1981), who found concentration to rise in the proportion of scientists and engineers per worker). Although R. & D. inputs are a noisy (to say the least) signal of innovative output, it is interesting that one can apparently observe the same type of effects on market structure when looking at both the inputs and the output of the innovative process. Finally, using a mixture of case-study and cross-section evidence, Mansfield (1984) found mixed evidence on the Blair hypothesis, observing a clear deconcentrating effect of innovation in drugs (but not in steel, petroleum, or chemicals). Carlsson (1984), on the other hand, found a marked deconcentrating effect in a case-study of metal-working. All in all, the effects of innovation on market structure observed on

since we are focusing on use and not the production of innovations, we have not distinguished process from product innovations, a decision at least partly due to the fact that many of the innovations in our data emerged from the engineering sector and, product or process, were user driven. New products that are not inputs into users' production processes may have effects on market structure analogous to those suggested by Blair, reducing concentration through their effect on product differentiation (say, by increasing horizontal differentiation and fragmenting markets).

Table 3.1 seem to be consistent with enough that is known from other studies to enable one to hazard the supposition that our results are not sample-specific.

Not surprisingly, concentration seems to be positively affected by capital intensity; changes in capital intensity also have a positive effect on C_t^* which, however, is difficult to discern accurately. Using the estimates of α_4 and α_5 from regression (ii), it turns out that the effect on ΔC_t^* of a change in K_{it} observed on average in the sample was roughly 40 per cent of that of $\Delta \tau_{it}$ in absolute magnitude. Hence, the increases in capital intensity observed in our data offset only part of the negative effect of the observed innovations $\Delta \tau_{it}$ on C_t^*.[10] Changes in market size effectively complete this offsetting, leaving $\Delta C_{it}^* \approx$ 0 on average.[11] Market size has a negative effect on C_t^* as expected, but this effect is extremely imprecisely measured. Similarly, the effect of changes in market size is also difficult to discern accurately, although it appears to be positive. All of these effects were also observed when K_{it} and Z_{it} were specified as beginning-year (i.e. 1970 and 1975) values rather than within-period averages (i.e. average values for 1970–4 and 1975–9).

The role of the fixed effects included in (7) is rather interesting. Recall that they have been included to control for a wide range of unobservable determinants of C_t^*, factors that must be taken into account when trying to assess the effects of those factors that can be observed. Regression (vi) presents estimates of (7) without the fixed effects. The restrictions that transform (ii) into (vi) are comfortably rejected at 1 per cent significance levels, but (vi) is very much closer to the kind of empirical model that is standard in the literature than (i)–(v). As can be seen, one can still observe a negative effect of $\Delta \tau_{it}$ on C_t^* in (vi), albeit slightly attenuated. Much the most dramatic effect of excluding fixed effects when they are, in fact, appropriate is observed in the estimate of γ_0, a matter we take up below. Still, to account for variations in the data is one thing, explaining them is quite another. That the fixed effects play a major role indicates that there is more to market-structure dynamics than

---

[10] Since technological advance will, in general, be embodied in new capital equipment, it is possible to argue that the net effect of innovation in market structure may possibly be somewhat overstated by α_5. In fact, $\Delta \tau_{it}$ and ΔK_{it} are not very highly correlated at all.

[11] The 10-year sample means are: $K_{it} = 1.665$, $\Delta K_{it} = .1407$, $Z_{it} = 5.966$, $\Delta Z_{it} = .286$, $\Delta \tau_{it} = 8.2397$, and $\Delta \tau_{it-1} = 6.3577$.

innovative activity, but, since these other contributing factors are not observable, one can make only limited progress in identifying the size of their impact. One can at least say something about observable factors which are either constant or can be observed only once over the period by comparing them with the estimates of the fixed effects, f_i. Retrieving the latter from equation (ii), we discovered them to be positively correlated to measures of minimum efficient scale and to measures of the capital required to build minimum efficient scale plants, but negatively correlated to advertising intensity in 1968. Thus, our data contain the same positive correlation between proxies for minimum efficient scale and concentration reported elsewhere in the literature, but contain a slight hint that advertising may be deconcentrating.

It is apparent from even the most cursory inspection of Table 3.1 that the fixed effects play a large role in determining the level of overall explanation achieved. Exactly the same results emerge if one regresses not ΔC_{it} but rather C_{it} on the right-hand side variables in (7) (nothing changes save the estimate of α_7), and both regressions indicate that the fixed effects play a major role in fixing estimates of C^*_{it}, the long-run equilibrium level of concentration in each industry. To appreciate what this means, consider the version of (7) with C_{it} as the dependent variable, and with $(1 + \alpha_7)$ as the coefficient on C_{it-1}. As a practical matter, the dominance of the fixed effects means that our data, like many other panel data-sets, exhibit far more variation across industries than over time. The implication would seem to be that C^*_{it} is relatively fixed over time but at different levels in each industry, and that C_{it} is close to C^*_{it}. This set of conjectures receives direct support from the results that $\Delta C^*_{it} \approx 0$ on average, that the fixed effects cannot be simplified into a single cross-industry constant, and that $\gamma_0 = 1$ (on this, see immediately below). Conditional on such industry-specific effects, the remaining estimated parameters in (7) rely on 'within-group' information, correlating movements in concentration over time in each industry (relative to the mean concentration level for each industry) to movements in innovative activity over time (relative to the industry mean innovation level). Interesting as this correlation is, the dominant role played by the fixed effects makes it plain that 'between-group' variation is of relatively more interest than this 'within-group' variation. That is, while innovations affect levels of concentration, the effect is small and does not induce major movements in C_{it} over time (or, at least, movements in C_{it} over t which are large relative to its variation across i).

Regression (ii) in Table 3.1 provides an estimate of $\gamma_0 = 1.08$, perhaps the most surprising result on the table at first sight. Most estimates of γ_0 reported in the literature have been much smaller, more nearly of the order of magnitude of that reported in regression (vi) in Table 3.1 (e.g. see the survey in Geroski and Masson, 1987). A little thought suggests that, despite being regularly reported, estimates like $\gamma_0 = .042$ reported in (vi) in Table 3.1 are rather difficult to accept; $\gamma_0 = 1$, on the other hand, is quite reasonable. The argument is as follows. Since the estimates of γ_0 in regressions (i)–(v) do not differ significantly from unity, they imply that the costs of adjusting market shares are small relative to the costs of being out of equilibrium. Although the expansion of market share through expanding old plants and building new ones is bound to be slow and costly, the fact of the matter is that most changes in concentration are driven by mergers. Whatever their effects on profits, mergers do enable firms to adjust their market shares quite rapidly. Accepting the result that γ_0 is much closer to zero than it is to unity has a profound effect on ones view about the dynamics of market structure, for it implies that C_t will never be far from C^*_t regardless of how large ΔC^*_t is. It follows that one must interpret the common observation that 'market structure is stable' as being true largely because C^*_t does not change very much over time. The hint that, if anything, γ_0 is slightly larger than unity implies that when C_{it} adjusts to changes in C^*_{it}, there is a very slight tendency to overshoot, and that C_{it} approaches C^*_{it} through a series of damped oscillations, which, in fact, are difficult to discern with any accuracy. By contrast, estimates of γ_0 on the order of magnitude of .042 paint quite a different picture. In this case, the implication is that the costs of adjusting shares is large, and so C_{it} may diverge from C^*_{it} for extended periods of time (e.g. see the simulations in Geroski and Masson, 1987). It follows that one must argue that 'market structure is stable' because agents react to changes in C^*_{it} with extreme lassitude. Although it is impossible to say a priori that adjustment must be quick, estimates like $\gamma_0 = .042$ suggest that it is so slow as to make the notion of a long-run target, C^*_{it}, practically worthless. This extreme conclusion is difficult to reconcile with virtually any reasonable a priori view, and leads one to believe that the estimates in (i)–(v) are far more reasonable than those reported in (vi) and most of the previous literature.[12]

Having said that the estimate $\gamma_0 = 1.08$ is more plausible than $\gamma_0 = .042$, does not, however, imply that one should uncritically argue that adjustment costs are unimportant. Adjustment costs are assumed to be convex in ΔC_{it}, and if one observes both large and small ΔC_{it}, then it ought be possible to get an accurate estimate of their size. If, however, one only observes rather small values of ΔC_{it}, then one will only have observations at the bottom (i.e. $\Delta C_{it} = 0$) and flat end of the adjustment cost function, observations that may lead one to think that such costs are zero when they are truly positive. Said differently, if $\Delta C^*_{it} = 0$, then $\Delta C_{it} = 0$ if costs of adjustment are low, and it is important not to confuse this state of affairs with that occasioned by small ΔC_{it} due to high adjustment costs. The bottom line appears to be that the costs of being out of equilibrium are probably larger than those of adjustment, and, with somewhat less confidence, that C_{it} will follow movements in C^*_{it} fairly quickly if not instantaneously.

Table 3.1 contains one final puzzle, and that is why our estimates of $\gamma_0 = 1.08$ depart so spectacularly from the estimates of γ_0 reported elsewhere in the literature. There are several possible explanations for this. Although many studies include a growth variable, most neglect the possibility that $\Delta C^*_{it} \neq 0$. Setting $\Delta \tau_{it} = \Delta Z_{it} = \Delta Z_{it} = 0$ simplifies regression (ii) in Table 3.1 to a regression of ΔC_{it} on C_{it-1}, K_{it} and Z_{it} and a full set of fixed effects. It turns out that this simpler model produces an estimate of $\gamma_0 = 1.081$, with Z_t negative and statistically significant and K_{it} positive and significant. Eliminating $\Delta \tau_{it}$ alone or ΔK_{it} and ΔK_{it} jointly or alone also has no effect on the estimate of γ_0. This leaves the fixed effects as the possible source of trouble, and the difference that they make is easily seen. Consider (7) where f_i is assumed to be fixed over time but different in each industry. Failure to measure f_i or, indeed, to measure it fully, clearly leads to an omitted variable bias. Since f_i and C_{it-1} are positively correlated across industries i, then the coefficient on C_{it-1} is likely to be biased upwards; i.e. that estimates of γ_0 are

---

[12] Geroski *et al.* (1987) estimated $C^* = 50.3$ for a sample of US industries for the period 1963–8, and most of the actual C_t were observed to be fairly near this figure. While one would be amazed were this not so, the point is that it is not a necessary implication of their model. For the UK in the period 1970–9, $C^* = .5142$ if $\Delta Z_{it} = \Delta K_{it} = 0$, and slightly larger at $C^* = .5241$ when ΔZ_{it} and ΔK_{it} are evaluated at their sample means.

likely to be biased downwards. Regression (vi) in Table 3.1, which replicates (ii) except that the fixed effects have been excluded, shows that this is exactly what happens. Thus, failure to fully model or, at least, to take account of variations in long-run equilibrium levels of concentration will lead to bias in estimating adjustment speeds. It appears from our calculations that previous work may have failed to fully capture variations in C^*_{it}, erroneously creating the impression of slow adjustment when, in fact, a fuller and more correctly specified model of C^*_{it} would have revealed that adjustment was generally rapid and, within a five-year period, usually more or less complete.[13]

4. *Final Reflections*

Market concentration has been gradually rising in the post-war period, largely propelled by at least two major merger waves (for the UK, see Hannah and Kay, 1977, and Hart and Clarke, 1980). Although mergers are clearly the major proximate cause of changes in concentration, they undoubtedly reflect the underlying reality of shifts in C^*_t and the need to adjust C_t to them. Our results suggest that adjustment of C_t is relatively rapid—not too surprising a result when it is carried out largely through merger—and that the consequent variation in concentration levels within industries over time is dwarfed by that between industries at any given time. Further, our results suggest that innovative activity does affect the evolution of market structure in particular industries, and that innovation plays a deconcentrating role wholly consistent with Blair's hypothesis about the decentralizing role of ninetieth-century innovations. However, the effects of innovation on market structure appear to be quantitatively small, and, in the UK of the 1970s, they were more or less exactly offset by increases in market size and capital intensity, producing very little net movement in long-run concentration levels on average.

One final remark is in order. Our results suggest that innovation reduces the level of concentration in markets, and that most of the impact of innovation on concentration occurs very quickly. There is, of course, a large literature which has focused on causal influences running from market structure to

---

[13] Much the same consequences of introducing fixed effects into dynamic models of industry profitability are recorded in Levy (1987).

innovativeness (e.g. see the surveys by Kamein and Schwartz, 1982, Scherer and Ross, 1990: ch. 15, Baldwin and Scott, 1987, and others), and it is worth integrating the two lines of enquiry. Geroski (1990), (reprinted as Chapter 4 in this volume, has presented results on the determinants of innovation rates for the UK in the same period which suggest that reductions in the level of market concentration increase innovativeness. Taken together, both sets of results point to a mutually reinforcing process in which innovations deconcentrate markets, and such deconcentration further stimulates innovative activity (*ceteris paribus*). While it certainly is possible to see in this a pattern of evolution consistent with Schumpeter's notion of 'creative destruction', it must also be said that the effects perceived in the data are not large in absolute magnitude.

Appendix

$\Delta \tau_{it}$ = number of major commercially successful innovations used in industry i. This data is based on a major study undertaken by SPRU, University of Sussex, of 4,378 major innovations in the UK, 1945–83; for details see Chapter 2 above. The data was obtained from the ESRC Data Archive at the University of Essex.

C_{it} = level of the five-firm concentration ratio. These data were unavailable for 1975, and we used the average value of 1974 and 1976. Repeating the regressions reported here using either 1974 or 1976, or using four-year changes in concentration produced virtually identical results.

Z_{it} and K_{it} = log of domestic industry production and the level of the capital stock–output ratio, the latter obtained from calculations made by Dick Allard for the Office of Fair Trading, and the former from the Census of Production. Domestic industry production is highly correlated with domestic sales (production less exports plus imports), and no substantive difference was made using either specification, nor when Z was defined as the level (rather than the log) of domestic production or sales.

4 Innovation, Technological Opportunity, and Market Structure*

1. *Introduction*

Discussions of the social cost of monopoly invariably end with a long list of caveats, of which the Schumpeterian hypothesis is perhaps the best known and most frequently invoked. The notion that monoply deadweight loss is the price that must be paid for high levels of innovative activity has attracted less support than attention, but still has enough adherents to ensure that it remains in the forefront of thinking about competition policy. The importance of the question demands that one examine the evidence available on the issue, and this chapter does so in the context of interindustry comparisons using cross-section data. (In what follows, we propose to explore the correlation between innovativeness and monopoly power by examining the effect of rivalry using more information on market structure than just concentration ratios, by correcting for interindustry variations in technological opportunity, and by distinguishing the effect that rivalry has on innovativeness for a given level of post-innovation returns from the effect that rivalry has on innovativeness through its effects on post-innovation returns.) Using data on major innovations introduced in the UK during the 1970s, we find fairly strong evidence

* First published in, and reprinted with the permission of, *Oxford Economic Papers*, 42 (1990): 586–602. I am obliged to D. Mueller, G. Stewart, J. Black, R. J. O'Brien, P. Stoneman, R. Pomroy, several referees, and to seminar participants at the Universities of Southampton, Exeter, Harvard, Cornell, Penn State, Bristol, Nottingham, the Economic Council of Canada, the Ministry of Finance in Paris, and Middlesex Polytechnic for useful comments. Jim Fairburn provided excellent research assistance. This research was supported by the ESRC, and parts of the data were obtained from the ESRC Data Archive in Essex and from the Business Statistics Office in Newport. Despite this debt, the usual disclaimer applies.

against the hypothesis that increases in competitive rivalry decrease innovativeness. That is, our data suggest that the price which has to be paid for high levels of innovation may not include tolerating the growth of highly concentrated, imperfectly competitive market structures.

The plan of the chapter is as follows. In Section 2, we briefly restate the Schumpeterian hypothesis, distinguishing three senses in which 'monopoly' may be thought to affect innovative activity. With this distinction in mind, Section 3 sets out a model for testing the Schumpeterian hypothesis and discusses its empirical implementation. Section 4 presents some empirical results for the UK, looking at the incidence of significant innovations during the period 1970–9 in seventy-three three-digit industries, and Section 5 contains a summary of the results.

2. *The Schumpeterian Hypothesis*

Popular versions of the Schumpeterian hypothesis contain several different assertions, but the one which we wish to focus on here is the argument that monopoly power stimulates innovative activity. To put this into a testable form, it is necessary to distinguish between *anticipated* and *actual* monopoly power (e.g. Kamien and Schwartz, 1982: 27). Anticipated monopoly power refers to an innovator's ability to enjoy the full benefits of its research by preventing imitation. Were the Schumpeterian hypothesis to be expressed solely in terms of the assertion that innovation occurs only when some degree of expected post-innovation monopoly ensures that the innovator will at least cover its costs, it would be relatively uncontroversial. Much more disputable are assertions about the effect of actual monopoly power. In principle, actual monopoly can have one or both of two effects on innovative activity: a *direct* effect for any given level of post-invention reward, and an *indirect* effect via the effect that actual monopoly has on the size of the post-innovation reward. Scherer (1980: 428–9) calls these the 'stimulus' and 'market room' factors.

An indirect effect of actual monopoly on innovative behaviour arises whenever current monopoly power affects the likelihood of achieving a given degree of post-innovation monopoly power. There are several reasons to suspect that this effect may be positive. Chief amongst these are the notions that a current-period monopolist will generally be well placed to erect barriers to future entry (e.g. Levin, 1978), and that the entry barriers which sustain a current-period monopoly position may be durable enough to protect the monopolist into the future. Further, whenever the results of future innovations complement innovations already made by the monopolist, then it will gain more than rivals will from their introduction and, if necessary, will pre-empt rivals (e.g. Gilbert and Newberry, 1982). Since it is difficult to imagine how actual monopoly might reduce expected post-innovation returns, the smallest indirect effect that one might plausibly expect is no effect at all.

The direct effect of actual monopoly on innovative behaviour is reflected in the response to a post-innovation return of any given size. Here it is possible to find plausible arguments that work in both directions (e.g. Scherer, 1980 : 423–38). A positive direct effect is expected by those who see monopolists as possessors of various types of material advantages. In particular, high current-period profits generated by the exercise of actual monopoly power may enable a monopolist to hire more highly qualified personnel, and may provide internal finance which facilitates a rapid response to events and weakens the firm's reliance on costly external finance. As against this, there are at least three reasons to expect a negative direct effect. First, the absence of active competitive forces may allow certain behavioural disadvantages of monopoly to become manifest. Managers may exhibit a preference for leisure or become sleepy, and bureaucratic inertia and control loss may generate substantial x-inefficiency. Second, increasing the number of firms searching for an innovation may raise the probability of getting it by some time t, either because the more firms there are undertaking research, the more intense is each firm's search activity, or because the more firms there are searching, the more likely it is that one will stumble upon the important clues by date t.[1] Finally, incumbent monopolists whose positions are based on previous innovations will enjoy a lower net return from introducing a new innovation which displaces part of the activities of the old one than entrants would (Arrow, 1962; see also Fellner, 1951). This opportunity cost of innovation compounds that which may arise if the incumbent's capital stock is locked into a particular technology, and slows the response of a monopolist

---

[1] The first of these propositions is a little controversial: compare Loury (1979) with Lee and Wilde (1980). On the second, see also Scherer (1967), Dasgupta and Stiglitz (1980*a*) and (1980*b*), Reinganum (1982), Futia (1980); Dasgupta (1986) and Kamien and Schwartz (1982), survey this material.

to a new innovation promising a positive return of any given size.

Thus, there are two effects of actual monopoly on innovative activity. While the indirect effect is likely to be positive, the direct effect may not be. To cast light on the size and direction of the overall effect of actual monopoly on innovative activity, it is necessary to try to isolate and measure the strength of each of these two effects taken separately. The empirical model to be discussed below is designed with precisely this goal in mind.

3. Model Specification

When examining the Schumpeterian hypothesis, it is natural to focus in the first instance on the relationship between actual market structure and research activity. There are a number of ways in which this relationship can be expressed, but most theoretical models suggest that research activity, S_i, will not occur if expected post-innovation returns, $\pi^e i$, are zero, and that research activity will increase as the level of such returns increases. Thus, we posit that

$$S_i = \theta_i(\pi^e_i)\alpha_1, \tag{1}$$

for industries indexed by i. Equation (1) has, in fact, appeared in the literature in at least two different guises. The first is in decision-theoretic models of where (1) is derived from the first-order conditions describing the choice of research intensity by each firm j and then summed over all j in i (e.g. Levin and Reiss, 1984; Stoneman, 1983: ch. 3; and others). (1) has also appeared as a zero-profit condition in several equilibrium models of rivalry (e.g. Loury, 1979, and others). In both cases, S_i is interpreted as research expenditure relative to sales, π^e_i as post-innovation price–cost margins, and θ_i generally depends on the degree of monopoly, M_i, and other factors, Z_i. As $\theta_i \geq 0$, it is natural to write

$$\log\theta_i = \alpha_0 + \alpha_2 M_i + \alpha_3 Z_i, \tag{2}$$

in which case,

$$\log S_i = \alpha_0 + \alpha_1 \log\pi^e_i + \alpha_2 M_i + \alpha_3 Z_i. \tag{3}$$

In terms of the discussion in Section 2, α_1 is the effect of anticipated monopoly on innovations, α_2 is the direct effect of actual monopoly, and $\alpha_1(\partial\log\pi^e/\partial M_i)$ is the indirect effect.

Regressions similar to (3) have appeared frequently in the literature, generally producing positive (but not always significant) correlations between R. & D. expenditures divided by sales (or, the proportion of scientists and engineers in the workforce) and industry concentration (e.g. see Scherer, 1980, Kamien and Schwartz, 1982, and Baldwin and Scott, 1987, for surveys). The problem with accepting these results as evidence consistent with the Schumpeterian hypothesis is that R. & D. expenditures are not only likely to be a poor measure of total research activity, but they may actually mismeasure true research activity with an error which depends on the degree of monopoly, M_i. If, as seems likely, R. & D. expenditures systematically understate the research activity of small firms and of putative entrants in competitive (i.e. 'low' M_i) industries, then estimates of α_1 will be biased upwards, and, indeed, estimated values of α_1 may be positive when the true value of α_1 is negative.[2] In these circumstances, it seems prudent to treat S_i as unobservable and look for an alternative method of measuring the direct and indirect effects of actual monopoly.

Since research activity will, sooner or later, produce an output in the form of one or more innovations, I_i, then one can still examine the Schumpeterian hypothesis despite the problems with (3) if one knows the relationship between research inputs and output, S_i and I_i. Any systematic association between the two can be exploited to replace the unobservable S_i by an indicator like I_i. In this context, it is natural to think (roughly) in terms of a production function $I_i = F(S_i)$, which exhibits diminishing returns (if only because of duplication in research across firms). Choosing a functional form largely on grounds of convenience, we assume that

$$I_i = \beta \log S_i + \mu_i, \tag{4}$$

---

[2] In partial support of this assertion, note that R. & D. expenditures are incurred almost exclusively by large firms whereas innovations are produced by large and small firms (e.g. Pavitt *et al.*, 1987, or Geroski and Stewart, 1991), suggesting that the research inputs of small firms are underrecorded (see also Kleinknecht (1987) for some direct evidence). This observation is also consistent with a range of studies which suggest that apparent research efficiency declines with firm size (e.g. Kamien and Schwartz, 1982: 66–70). Part of the problem seems to be that small firms generally do different types of research from large ones, and much of it is less formal and less tied to R. & D. labs than is true in large firms; Pavitt *et al.* (1987) also observe that the research of small firms is often supported by the users of innovations in other industries. Putative entrants who do research but fail to enter are also not recorded in industry R. & D. totals.

where μ_i, the 'propensity to innovate' (adapting a term introduced by Scherer, 1965; see also Pakes, 1985), reflects other
exogenous factors above and beyond research inputs, S_i, which
generate innovations (including simple luck, good or bad). Using
(4) to eliminate S_i in (3) yields

$$I_i = \gamma_0 + \gamma_1 \log\pi^e_i + \gamma_2 M_i + \gamma_3 Z_i + \mu_i, \tag{5}$$

where the γ_k, $k = 0, 1, 2, 3$ are proportional to the α_k, being
scaled up by a positive constant β. Hence, $\gamma_2 < 0$ points to a
negative direct effect of actual monopoly on innovation, and, if
$\partial\log\pi^e_i / \partial M_i > 0$, then $\gamma_1 > 0$ points to a positive indirect effect;
the total effect is proportional to the quantity $(\gamma_2 + \gamma_1 \partial\log\pi^e_i / \partial M_i)$.

Thus, (5) is a model which enables one to chart the direction
and measure relative size of the two effects of actual monopoly
on innovation without needing to measure research inputs
accurately.[3] Given (5) as an empirical vehicle, there are four specification decisions to consider. These translate the variables
on the right-hand side of (5) into observables, and we consider
each in turn.

The first specification decision concerns $\log\pi^e_i$, the level of
price–cost margins expected post-innovation. Being an expectation, $\log\pi^e_i$ is not directly observable, and must be proxied.
Two courses of action suggest themselves. The simplest path to
follow is to assume that agents have complete foresight, i.e. to
take expected post-innovation margins to equal actual, observed
post-innovation margins. Alternatively, one might assume that
agents do not possess complete foresight, but do form rational
expectations derived from a model of how innovations affect
industry profitability. If the log of expected price–cost margins
depends linearly on innovative output, I_i, monopoly M_i, and
other factors, W_i, then the assumption of rational expectations
means that the log of observed price–cost margins, π_i, is given
by

$$\log\pi_i = \tilde{N}_0 + \tilde{N}_1 I_i + \tilde{N}_2 M_i + \tilde{N}_3 W_i + \varepsilon_i, \tag{6}$$

---

[3] Measuring I_i inaccurately does not have the same impact on Schumpeterian tests
as errors in measuring S_i do. To see this, suppose that the total output of research is
$I_i + J_i$, of which only I_i is observed. If $I_i = \beta_1 \log S_i + \mu^1_i$ and $J_i = \beta_2 \log S_i + \mu^2_i$, then $(I_i + J_i) = \beta_3 \log S_i + \mu^3_i$, where $\beta_3 \equiv \beta_1 + \beta_2$ and $\mu^3_i \equiv \mu^1_i + \mu^2_i$. It is clear that regressing I_i
on S_i gives a biased estimate of β_3 (although estimates of β_1 are unbiased), but neither
β_1 nor β_3 are associated with the Schumpeterian hypothesis. That is, as α_1 and α_3 are
observed up to the same factor of proportionality in (5), testing for their relative size
is unaffected by any bias involved in estimating that factor of proportionality.

where $\varepsilon_i \equiv \log\pi_i - \log\pi^e_i$ is a classical regression error. Following standard procedures and using the predictions from a reduced-form regression of $\log\pi_i$ on M_i, W_i, and Z_i to proxy $\log\pi^e_i$ in (5) enables one to generate consistent, if inefficient, estimates of the γ_k.[4]

The second specification decision concerns measuring the degree of monopoly, M_i. The usual practice in the literature is to proxy this using an index of concentration, effectively hanging the test for direct effects on a single coefficient. This seems somewhat restrictive. The degree of rivalry in a market is difficult to determine with any precision, and probably cannot be completely captured by just one variable. To avoid the problems that trying to do this might create (and choosing to err (if at all) on the side of excessive inclusion), we have used six measures of rivalry: the extent of market penetration by entrants (*ENTRY*), the market share of imports (*IMPORT*), the relative number of small (less than ninety-nine employees) firms (*SFIRM*), the within-period percentage change in concentration (*DCON*), the market share of exiting firms (*EXIT*), and the five-firm market concentration ratio (*CON*).[5] An industry with extensive entry, an active small-firm sector, a low and falling concentration ratio, and low exit has many of the structural features that one normally associates with 'competitive' markets. By contrast, low entry, a small and contracting fringe sector, and a high and rising level of market concentration are all likely to be features of monopolistic markets in which 'rivalry' is weak. Hence, we shall interpret positive coefficients

---

[4] On estimating rational-expectations models, see Wallis (1980) and Wickens (1982). One might insist that the relevant post-entry return be that increment in returns attributable to innovations (as stressed e.g. by Futia, 1980). Denoting the expected number of innovations as I^e_i, then replacing $\log\pi^e_i$ by $\psi_1 I^e_i$ changes (5) to $I_i = \gamma_0 + (\gamma_1\psi)I^e_i + \gamma_2 M_i + \gamma_3 Z_i + \mu_i$. Assuming for the moment that μ_i is purely random and has zero mean, then, taking expectations and solving, $I^e_i = (1 - \gamma_1\psi)^{-1}(\gamma_0 + \gamma_2 M_i + \gamma_3 Z_i)$, and so $I_i = h_0 + h_1 M_i + h_2 Z_i + \mu_i$, say. Thus, interpreting $\log\pi^e_i$ as not price–cost margins but as the increment of returns attributable to expected innovations reduces (5) to a linear relationship between I_i, M_i, Z_i, and μ_i, and changes slightly the interpretation of the γ_k. The main problem with this is that it is no longer possible to separately identify direct and indirect effects. None of the remarks to be made below about estimates of γ_2 calculated from our data is affected by omitting proxies for $\log\pi^e_i$ from the estimating equation.

[5] In support of including the entry and small-firm variables, see Beesley and Hamilton (1984) who stress the 'seed bed' role of new firms, associating industry innovative activity with high 'turbulence' or turnover. The role of small firms and entrants in stimulating innovativeness and diffusion, particularly at various stages of the industry life-cycle, is discussed in empirical work by Gort and Klepper (1982), Abernathy and Utterback (1975), and Kaplinsky (1983), and is attested to in numerous case-studies; see also Comanor (1967) on the role of entry barriers. The variable *DCON* is intended to reflect the activities of established fringe firms challenging the leading five.

on the first three variables (*ENTRY, IMPORT, SFIRM*) and negative ones on the last three (*DCON, EXIT, CON*) as consistent with a negative direct effect of actual monopoly on innovation.

In addition to rivalry, there are a number of further factors which may affect the speed with which industries with a given degree of monopoly respond to changes in post-innovation returns. The third specification decision is concerned with these added factors, the Z_i. None of these factors is of interest *per se* in the present exercise, their inclusion being determined by trade-offs between inefficiency (inclusion of irrelevant variables) or bias (exclusion of relevant variables correlated to M_i) in the estimation of γ_1 and γ_2. We have included five such conditioning variables: industry size and growth (*SIZE, GROW*), capital intensity (**KAYO**), export intensity (*EXPORT*), and a proxy for industry unionization (*UNION*). Of these, *UNION, SIZE,* and *KAYO* are known to be highly correlated to M_i, while *GROW* and *EXPORT* are obvious inclusions given previous empirical work in this area. While it has not proved possible to collect enough variables to encompass all the Schumpeterian regressions reported in the literature, this group of variables takes us most of the way.

Last but by no means least in (5) is the propensity to innovate, μ_i, which summarizes the numerous exogenous factors which affect the average productivity of research, I_i/S_i.[6] Chief amongst these are the conditions of supply which facilitate or inhibit the generation of innovations, conditions sometimes referred to as 'technological opportunity' (e.g. Scherer, 1965, or Levin *et al.*, 1985; Rosenberg, 1974, is a classic discussion of the importance of these factors). Previous work in this area has followed a variety of different routes in modelling differences in technological opportunity across industries in terms of observables, none of them completely satisfactory.[7] We differ

---

[6] One might consider allowing the propensity to innovate to affect the marginal productivity of research by writing (4) as $\log I_i = \beta \log S_i + \mu_i$, say. (5) then would have $\log I_i$ as its dependent variable, but all else would remain the same. Testing whether the propensity to innovate affects the marginal product would, in these circumstances, amount to testing whether I_i or $\log I_i$ is the appropriate dependent variable in (5). As it happens, our data are poorly described by a model with $\log I_i$ as the dependent variable.

[7] Thus e.g. Lunn and Martin (1983) and Scherer (1965) use a few subjectively selected industry dummies; Waterson and Lopez (1983) use a proxy for capital intensity and changes in productivity; Schrieves (1978) uses information on types of scientists and engineers in firms; Hughes (1984) uses foreign R. & D. intensity; and Levin *et al.* (1985) use a variety of measures which proxy closeness to science, the sources of technical progress, industry maturity, conditions of appropriability, and so on.

from much of this literature in not trying to model technological opportunity in terms of observables, a procedure which,
however desirable in principle, is, in practice, plagued by problems arising from the omission of relevant factors which are
difficult to observe. Instead, we take our cue from the observation that technological opportunity is not only exogenous to
current-period research decisions, but is also likely to be relatively constant in the short to medium run. Hence, while it
takes a specific value for each industry, it is constant over time
industry by industry. Thus, we write μ_i as containing two components: 'technological opportunity', τ_i, an industry-specific
constant, and η_i, a zero-mean normally distributed random
variable capturing 'all other factors'.

The consequence of all the decisions discussed in this section
is the regression model

$$
\begin{aligned}
I_i = f_i &+ \lambda_1 \log\pi^e_i + \lambda_2\, CON_i \\
&+ \lambda_3\, ENTRY_i + \lambda_4\, IMPORT_i + \lambda_5\, SFIRM_i \\
&+ \lambda_6\, EXIT_i + \lambda_7\, DCON_i + \lambda_8\, SIZE_i \\
&+ \lambda_9\, GROW_i + \lambda_{10}\, DATA_i + \lambda_{11}\, EXPORT_i \\
&+ \lambda_{12}\, DCON_i + \eta_i,
\end{aligned}
\tag{7}
$$

where $\log\pi^e_i$ can be proxied either by $\log\pi_i$ or by an instrument
derived from (6), and $f_i \equiv \tau_i\gamma_0$. The sign pattern: $\lambda_3, \lambda_4, \lambda_5 > 0$ and
$\lambda_2, \lambda_6, \lambda_7 < 0$ will be interpreted as a negative direct effect of
monopoly on innovation, and the pattern $\lambda_3, \lambda_4, \lambda_5 < 0$ and λ_2,
$\lambda_6, \lambda_7 > 0$ as a positive effect. λ_1 is the effect of anticipated
monopoly on innovation. Each of the six rivalry variables have
an effect on $\log\pi^e_i$ given by (6), say $\phi_{21}, \ldots \phi_{26}$. Thus the indirect
effects on innovation associated with them are $\lambda_1\phi_{11}, \ldots \lambda_1\phi_{16}$,
with total effects $(\lambda_2 + \lambda_1\phi_{11}), \ldots, (\lambda_7 + \lambda_1\phi_{16})$. These will be the
parameters of interest in the estimation which follows.

4. Results

The basic data that we have used are information on 4,378
significant innovations produced and used in the UK, 1945–83.
Given the need to estimate fixed effects, we focused on two 73
MLH (or, three-digit) industry cross-section panels covering the
periods 1970–4 and 1975–9, using average values over the five-
year period for the independent variables (for further details,

see the Appendix).[8] The dependent variable, I_i, is non-negative and so a Tobit estimator was used, producing the estimates shown in Table 6.1.

Column (i) in Table 4.1 shows our preferred estimates, using a rational expectations proxy for $\log\pi^e_i$. Column (ii) uses the log of actual post-innovation margins, and a comparison between the two suggests that the precise specification of $\log\pi^e_i$ has very little qualitative effect on the results.[9] Both columns (i) and (ii) assume that the eleven remaining variables are exogenous, and we have adopted this as a maintained hypothesis for $SIZE_i$, $GROW_i$, $KAYO_i$, $EXPORT_i$, and $UNION_i$. However, since the endogeneity of market structure is an integral element of Schumpeterian notions of 'creative destruction' (Levin and Reiss (1984) and Dasgupta (1986) each make this case in slightly different ways), it is important to test the exogeneity assumptions made on the six rivalry variables. Tests conducted on the six considered jointly, singly, and on numerous subsets of the six all uniformly indicated a failure to reject the null of exogeneity, although in the case of CON_i the decision was close to marginal.[10] Column (iii) shows 2SLS estimates of the same model as column (i) when CON_i is assumed to be endogenous. Although the indications are that the value of λ_2 in column (i) may be biased upwards somewhat, there seems to be little doubt that the true value of $\lambda_2 < 0$. Finally, it is worth remarking that the standard errors reported in all three columns have probably

[8] The innovations database only provides 80 possible MLH industry classifications, and 7 further industries were eliminated because of holes in our capital-stock series. The number of innovations produced in each period were 538 and 665 respectively; 27 and 16 industries in each sample recorded no innovations; the maximum number of innovations per sector was 88 and 134, both in sector 354 (Industrial Engines). Five-year intervals were chosen to minimize the effect of any inaccuracies in recording the precise date of innovation.

[9] The rational expectations proxy for $\log\pi^e_i$ was generated as the predictions of a reduced-form regression of margins on lagged innovations, lagged innovations squared, growth, exports, unionization, risk (the within-period standard deviation of price–cost margins), capital–output ratio, capital expenditures, industry size squared, and a full set of fixed effects. Including the six rivalry variables in the set of regressors had very little substantive effect, and, indeed, numerous experiments with this set of exogenous variables suggested that the qualitative features of the estimates of λ_1 in Table 4.1 are reasonably robust. Much the same applies for a model involving the level rather than the log of π^e_i, and for a model in which π_i is profits on assets rather than price–cost margins.

[10] See Smith and Blundell (1986) for an extension of the Wu test (Wu, 1973) to the Tobit model. The instruments used were those used for $\log\pi^e_i$ (see n. 9 above). It is noticeable that lagged (i.e. pre-1970) innovations had a clear negative influence on current levels of concentration, a correlation that is explored more fully in Geroski and Pomroy, 1990 (repr. as Ch. 3 in this volume).

Table 4.1 Regression results for equation (7)

Independent variables (means)	(i)	(ii)	(iii)	(iv)	(v)
$\log\pi_i$ (−.588)	2.27* (.146)	1.16 (.176)	11.54* (.72)	4.20 (.897)	21.96* (3.70)
CON_i (.517)	−58.42 (2.34)	−57.57 (2.27)	−439.2* (2.42)	−50.87 (3.05)	7.12 (.695)
$ENTRY_i$ (.05)	18.40 (1.05)	18.51 (1.05)	25.28 (1.44)	31.864 (1.94)	41.03 (.780)
$IMPORT_i$ (.213)	−.401 (.129)	−.380 (.122)	−.102 (.033)	−2.14 (.239)	10.43 (.941)
$SFIRM_i$ (.738)	3.63 (1.09)	3.61 (1.09)	4.94 (1.49)	12.46 (2.13)	−15.73 (1.09)
$EXIT_i$ (.049)	−25.94 (1.36)	−26.17 (1.38)	−25.28 (1.34)	−18.03 (2.207)	59.45 (1.28)
$DCON_i$ (.013)	−10.01 (2.22)	−0.73 (2.02)	−10.75 (2.35)	−7.68 (2.24)	−20.08 (1.42)
$SIZE_i$ (5.76)	4.24 (.614)	4.27 (.625)	−6.16 (.724)	.071 (.016)	8.51 (3.45)
$GROW_i$ (.742)	3.46 (1.91)	3.44 (1.91)	5.36 (2.58)	2.30 (2.06)	1.14 (.246)
$KAYO_i$ (1.66)	.854 (1.26)	.835 (1.25)	2.19 (2.37)	.906 (1.75)	−4.36 (3.66)
$EXPORT_i$ (.295)	6.84 (.857)	6.98 (.883)	33.5 (2.26)	4.01 (.916)	16.56 (2.77)
$UNION_i$ (.778)	−2.618 (.489)	−2.615 (.911)	−4.922 (1.00)	−7.77 (1.77)	−16.417 (1.02)
$\log L$	−309.82	−309.82	−309.63	−392.58	−462.90

* = instrumented (for details, see nn. 9 and 10).

Notes: Equations (i)–(iii) are Tobit estimates that include fixed effects; values of δ from the Tobit were: 4.38 (13.9), 4.38 (13.9), and 4.38 (13.9), respectively (*t*-values in brackets); equation (iv) duplicates (ii) using OLS, while (v) duplicates (i) suppressing the fixed effects into a single constant common to all industries; *t*-values (in absolute value) are in brackets below estimated coefficients. The definition of the variables is: I_i = number of innovations; CON_i = 5-firm concentration ratio; $GROW_i$ = per cent change in domestic production over the period; $SIZE_i$ = log of industry capital stock; $DCON_i$ = per cent change in industry concentration; $KAYO_i$ = capital–output ratio; $IMPORT_i$ = imports as a per cent of sales; $ENTRY_i$ = market share of entrants in year of entry; $EXPORT_i$ = exports as a per cent of sales; $SFIRM_i$ = no. firms ≤ 99 employees as a per cent of total number of firms; $EXIT_i$ = market share of exiting firms in the year of exit; $UNION_i$ = per cent of the workforce covered by collective agreements, and $\log\pi^e_i$ = expected post–innovation price–cost margins.

been inflated by the perhaps excessive inclusion of variables given the extent of collinearity that exists between them. $IMPORT_i$ and $EXPORT_i$, CON_i and $UNION_i$, $KAYO_i$ and $SIZE_i$, CON_i and $SIZE_i$, and $ENTRY_i$ and $EXIT_i$ are all noticeably positively correlated, while CON_i and $SFIRM_i$, CON_i and $ENTRY_i$, and CON_i and $EXIT_i$ are negatively correlated. It is, of course, not terribly surprising to discover that these variables contain similar information, and it is not surprising to discover that columns (i)–(iii) can be simplified in numerous ways by excluding subsets of the twelve independent variables. However, with the exception of simplifications which exclude $KAYO_i$ and/or $SIZE_i$, parameter estimates were extremely robust to such simplifications; exclusion of $KAYO_i$ and $SIZE_i$ did have noticeable effects on some coefficient sizes, but not on any signs. Needless to say, t-statistics were generally higher in more parsimonious representations.

The estimates reported in columns (i)–(iii) all provide fairly strong evidence that is inconsistent with the notion that there is a positive direct effect of actual monopoly on innovativeness. Only λ_4 violates the sign pattern identified earlier as corresponding to a negative direct effect, and this coefficient is insignificant. λ_2 and λ_7 are both negative and significant, λ_6 is negative, and λ_3 and λ_5 are positive. Thus, it seems to be the case that highly concentrated industries and those in the process of becoming more concentrated are less innovative than more competitive-looking ones (given the level of post-innovation returns, $\log \pi^e_i$), and there is a noticeable tendency for this to be true for industries subject to high net entry rates,[11] and for industries which have a large small-firm sector. Anticipated monopoly, as captured by $\log \pi^e_i$, has a positive effect on innovativeness, but it is an effect that is extremely difficult to estimate with precision. Industry size, export intensity, and unionization all appear to be relatively unrelated to innovativeness (although with exports, this is not completely clear), while growth and capital intensity are positively associated with innovativeness (albeit weakly). Both Tobit and OLS predictions from (i)–(iii) were quite accurate, and OLS regressions produced R^2's in the range of 90–5 per cent. One concludes from (i)–(iii) that increases in rivalry and reductions in monopoly market power increase innovativeness for a given level of post-innovation return, π^e_i.

---

[11] The restriction $\lambda_3 = -\lambda_6$ is statistically acceptable, suggesting that it is net entry (rather than gross entry) which has an impact on innovativeness.

These results are also robust to the method of estimation used. Comparisons between the estimates in column (i) and those generated using a linear method revealed that, while some bias exists in the latter because of the censored dependent variable, that bias does not substantively affect the features of (i)–(iii) just remarked upon.[12] Tobit estimates are, however, not always robust to apparently minor misspecifications, and the choice between Tobit and least squares or instrumental variable estimates is not necessarily straightforward. Column (iv) in Table 4.1 reproduces column (ii) using OLS and shows that the choice is, in this case, not controversial. Re-estimating (i) and (iii) by instrumental variables (not shown) leads to much the same conclusion. The Tobit model is of course, based on the rather strong assumption that increases in the independent variables have the same effect on the probability of limit observations as on the density of non-limit ones. So-called 'double hurdle' models relax this assumption (e.g. see Blundell and Meghir, 1987), and, when applied to our data, suggest that CON_i has little effect on the probability that an innovation will be produced and/or adopted in industry i, but has a strong negative effect on the number of innovations adopted that were generated elsewhere (given that at least one innovation was adopted or generated in i), and a weak positive effect on the probability that an innovation generated elsewhere and adopted in i will be adopted in i by a new entrant (who presumably uses it as a vehicle of entry) and not an established incumbent. Thus, the result that $\lambda_2 < 0$ seems to reflect not so much the reluctance of monopolists to innovate as to a reluctance to extensively innovate when they do innovate, and a slowness in generating innovation which is more than matched by an unwillingness to adopt innovations generated elsewhere. The consequence of all of this is that entry by outsiders bearing new innovations is more likely in monopolistic industries, and plays an important role in keeping them technically progressive.

The principal problem with columns (i)–(iii) is not so much interpreting the pattern of signs observed as reconciling them with results reported in previous empirical studies. Most of these have focused on the role of CON_i alone among the rivalry variables, and almost all of them have suggested that $\lambda_2 > 0$. In fact, the resolution of this particular conundrum turns out to

[12] I_i is, of course, an integer, but we have not explored models of count data (e.g. Hausman *et al.*, 1984, and Cameron and Trivedi, 1966) since more than 20 per cent of the sample had values of $I_i \geq 10$, and 10 per cent had $I_i \geq 20$.

depend on the treatment of technological opportunity. If, as is generally, believed, technological opportunity is higher in more concentrated sectors, then failing to completely capture its interindustry variation will lead estimates of λ_2 to be biased upward.[13] If this is so, then the relatively complete correction that a fixed-effects model provides ought to yield an estimate of λ_2 close to its true value. Further, if other types of correction for technological opportunity are incomplete, then it is possible that positive values of λ_2 will be observed when, in fact, the true value of λ_2 is negative, as reported in Table 4.1. This is an assertion which is easily tested, since the simplification of (7) which embodies the hypothesis that technological opportunity is the same in all sectors is an equation without fixed effects but with a constant whose value is common to all sectors. Column (v) in Table 4.1 reports estimates of (i) which embody this (statistically unacceptable) simplification (estimates of (ii) and (iii) suppressing the fixed effects lead to qualitatively similar conclusions). It is clear at a glance that neglecting technological opportunity produces estimates of λ_2 that are not only badly biased, but are so biased as to suggest that this one factor alone may account for the difference between columns (i)–(iii) and previous results. That is, as (v) replicates the major feature in question of previous work, then one is entitled to hazard the conjecture that our results are not sample- or data-specific. Rather, it seems to be the case that the usual methodology of testing the Schumpeterian hypothesis contains a flaw which imparts a distinctly 'pro-Schumpeterian' bias to the results.[14]

---

[13] Most scholars have not questioned the existence of a positive correlation between monopoly and technological opportunity (e.g. Scherer, 1980: 435), although the reasons vary according to the particular interpretation of technological opportunity favoured by particular authors. Two examples are: (i) technological opportunity may reflect government-supported, defence-related research which, in the UK, is highly concentrated in the hands of a few large firms in highly concentrated industries; and (ii) it may also reflect ease of appropriability and so be correlated to π^e_i and thus to M_i through the correlation between these two.

[14] This result is not new, although it is more dramatic than most reported in the literature. Most previous studies report that the introduction of variables intended to correct for variations in technological opportunity reduces the sign and significance of λ_2 (e.g. Scherer, 1965). The Cohen *et al.* (1987) exploration of the firm size–R. & D. link reports results with very similar features to those discussed above; that is, technological opportunity seems to play a central role and failing to take this into account appears to exaggerate the pro-Schumpeterian features of the data. As in Levin *et al.* (1985), this study also reports much progress in modelling technological opportunity, using observables accounting for about 50 per cent of its apparent interindustry variation. Although mitigating the bias created by ignoring technological opportunity, this only partially successful correction does not eliminate it.

The comparison between columns (i)–(iii) and (v) casts some interesting light on the role played by technological opportunity in accounting for interindustry variations in innovativeness. It is clear that the conditions of technological opportunity are highly correlated with many of the twelve independent variables in (7) and, indeed, a regression of estimates of the fixed effects on these twelve for either subperiod produces an R^2 slightly in excess of 50 per cent. Furthermore, industries with high technological opportunity appear not only to be highly concentrated (and relatively unfavourable to small firms), but also to be large, not very capital-intensive, and rather more profitable than the rest. These sectors also seem to experience higher domestic and foreign entry. As a consequence, failing to correct for technological opportunity leads one to substantially overstate the effect of anticipated monopoly on innovativeness (λ_1), incorrectly sign the effects of concentration, imports, small firms, and exit (λ_2, λ_4, λ_5, λ_6), exaggerate the effect of market size and unionization (λ_8, λ_{12}), understate that of growth (19), exaggerate the significance of exports (λ_{11}), and mistakenly attribute a retarding influence to capital intensity on innovation. Finally, it appears to be the case that variations in technological opportunity taken alone account for at least 60 per cent of the variation in innovations, while the twelve observables in (7) account, at best, for about 30 per cent.[15] Thus, technological opportunity not only appears to be the dominant influence in innovativeness, it also colours the role that more conventional observable factors appear to play.

Thus, it appears that actual monopoly has an inhibiting direct effect on innovativeness. However, while rivalry may increase innovativeness by increasing the response to a given level of $\log \pi^e_i$, increases in rivalry may also indirectly lower innovativeness by reducing $\log \pi^e_i$. To assess the size of this indirect and potentially offsetting effect, it is necessary to estimate (6). This type of equation is familiar from the literature

---

[15] The problem with decomposing the variation in innovations into that associated with technological opportunity and that associated with the rest of (7) is the high correlation between these two. OLS variants of (v) yielded R^2's no higher than 30 per cent, while OLS variants of (1)–(iii) yielded R^2's no lower than 90 per cent, leaving a minimum contribution by technological opportunity of 60 per cent or so. It is possible that the true figure may be as high as 75–80 per cent. Results emphasizing the major role played by technological opportunity imply that interindustry variations in innovativeness will be rather stable over time, an observation which is consistent with failure to reject the null of parameter variation between the two cross-section panels estimated separately.

(e.g. see the survey by Schmalensee, 1989), and, as a series of experiments suggested that the results on indirect effects are not sensitive to the precise details of its specification, we can be brief. Column (i) in Table 4.2 shows an equation in which the six rivalry variables, the five additional variables in (7), two additional exogenous variables, and fixed effects are added to an instrument for I_i to explain $\log \pi_i$.[16] Although collinearity has inflated estimates of standard errors, it seems fairly plain that, in broad terms, monopoly increases and rivalry reduces price–cost margins. The effect of concentration is positive but declining; entry, imports, changes in concentration, and small firms all have negative effects, and exit has a positive effect on margins. In short, since rivalry appears to reduce margins, the potential exists for the indirect effects of actual monopoly on innovation to offset its direct effect. The rest of the estimates of (6) are, on the whole, not inconsistent with what one might expect. Risk and innovations have a positive effect on margins, size, growth, and capital intensity negative ones, and exports and unionization have extremely weak positive effects that, like the imports effect, are almost certainly insignificant. Virtually identical qualitative results were observed in an equation whose dependent variable was π_i rather than $\log \pi_i$.

Column (ii) in Table 4.2 shows the direct effects taken from column (i) in Table 4.1, although, as will be plain in a moment, one could use the estimates from columns (ii)–(iii) in Table 4.1and find virtually the same results. Column (iii) in Table 4.2 shows estimates of the indirect effects using $\lambda_1 = 2.27$ from (i) in Table 4.1 and evaluating the indirect effect of concentration at its mean, $\overline{CON}_i = .51$. Even if one used $\lambda_1 = 11.54$ from (iii) in Table 4.1, it is still easy to see that the direct effects dwarf the indirect effects for all eleven variables in Table 4.2. The indirect effects of entry, small firms, exit, industry, size, growth, capital intensity, and unionization mildly offset the direct effects on innovation associated with these variables, and those of concentration (at the mean), imports, changes in concentration, and exports weakly reinforce their direct effects. Column (iv) in Table 4.2 shows the total effects of each of the eleven

[16] The instrument is derived from an OLS regression of I_i on fixed effects, lagged I_i, lagged I_i squared, growth, exports, the six rivalry variables, unionization, risk (the within-period standard deviation of price–cost margins), capital intensity, capital expenditures, size, and size squared. The results reported in Table 4.2 are robust to numerous alterations in this specification. The system defined by this equation (which is a reduced form) and (6) as it appears in column (i) of Table 4.2 is over-identified.

Table 4.2 Regression results for equation (6) and the calculation of direct and indirect effects

Variables	(i)	(ii)	(iii)	(iv)
CON_i	.323 (.270)	−58.42	−.499	−58.919
$ENTRY_i$	−.838 (2.56)	18.40	−1.890	16.51
$IMPORT_i$	−.0049 (.017)	−.401	−.011	−.412
$SFIRM_i$	−.260 (1.87)	3.63	−.5902	3.37
$EXIT_i$	.445 (1.48)	−25.94	1.010	−24.93
$DCON_i$	−.102 (1.20)	−10.01	−.231	−10.241
$SIZE_i$	−.239 (1.71)	4.24	−.542	3.698
$GROW_i$	−.056 (1.81)	3.46	−.127	3.333
$KAYO_i$	−.017 (1.30)	.854	−.038	.816
$EXPORT_i$	.020 (.139)	6.84	.045	6.885
$UNION$	.040 (.234)	−2.61	.09	−2.52

The dependent variable in (i) is $\log \pi_i$, and (i) also includes fixed effects, $RISK_i$ = 1.17 (1.32), an instrument for I_i = .0159 (3.59), and CON_i squared = −.806 (.704). $RISK_i$ is measured as the standard deviation of price–cost margins within the relevant five-year period. The R^2 for this equation = .973, F(85, 59) = 25.0363, the number of observations = 146, and SSR = .4044. The equation was estimated by OLS and the estimates are heteroscedastic-consistent; the absolute value of t-statistics is given in brackets. Column (ii) gives the direct effects taken from (i) in Table 4.1, column (iii) gives the indirect effects calculated from the coefficient in $\log \pi_i$ in (i) in Table 4.1 (the indirect effect for CON_i is evaluated at the mean, $\overline{CON_i}$ = .51) and the numbers on (ii) in 4.2, and, finally, column (iv) shows the total effects of actual monopoly on innovation.

variables on innovativeness, and it is apparent that the total effects are not only of the same sign, but virtually of the same size as the direct effects. In these circumstances, it seems reasonable to conclude that actual monopoly has an unambiguously inhibiting effect, and that rivalry has an unambiguously stimulating effect on innovativeness.

5. *Conclusions*

Our goal in this chapter has been to cast light on the hypothesis that rivalry is inimical and monopoly conducive to innovativeness. The test itself is not completely straightforward since monopoly can, in principle, have both an indirect effect via post-innovation returns and a direct effect given the level of post-innovation returns. Our examination of these effects used conventional interpretations of six rather imperfect measures of rivalry, and sought to discern a specific pattern of signs in the data. The calculations revealed that monopoly appears to inhibit the response to a given level of post-innovation returns, and that the indirect effects on innovativeness are relatively small. There is, in short, almost no support in the data for popular Schumpeterian assertions about the role of actual monopoly in stimulating progressiveness.

This set of results carries strong implications for policy as well as for future empirical research. On the policy front, one is entitled to be sceptical about the wisdom of industrial policies which seek to promote progressiveness by creating 'national champions'. Monopolies, whether publicly or privately created, do not seem to be particularly progressive in general, and it is hard to believe that restraining the hand of anti-trust authorities will improve this picture. Small firms and new entrants play a role in stimulating innovativeness which is clearly discernible in the data, and probably considerably understates their total effect on innovation. Competition—desirable on other grounds—certainly seems desirable in this area too. The next step for research also seems obvious. While we have been able to correct for variations in technological opportunity, its importance demands that much more attention be paid to modelling it, and to identifying the factors which seem to be important components of it. The role of rivalry in stimulating innovation is interesting, but it is apparently nowhere near as important as that of technological opportunity.

Data Appendix

I_i = number of significant technically and commercially successful innovations used in industry i. These data are based on a major study (involving 400 experts) by SPRU, University of Sussex, of 4,378 major innovations in the UK, 1945–83; for details see Chapter 2 above. Explicit attempts were made to overcome a natural tendency to concentrate on large firms and, although it is extremely unlikely, this may have imported a slight tendency to exaggerate the contribution of smaller firms. It is not clear that such a bias, if present, would have much effect on our conclusions about monpoly power, since highly concentrated markets may be composed of firms small in absolute size and large firms that operate in very large markets may have only modest market shares in these markets. The data were obtained from the ESRC Data Archive at Essex.

π_i = price–cost margins, defined as net output less the wage bill less net capital expenditure divided by gross output. Data were obtained from the Census of Production.

DCON and CON_i = percentage change and level of the five-firm concentration ratio, from the Census of Production.

$ENTRY_i$ and $EXIT_i$ = market share of all new firms and of exiting firms. The data were drawn from a special compilation made by the Business Statistics Office. *ENTRY* and *EXIT* for the 1970–4 period were measured by 1974 values of the variables since data for 1970–3 were not available.

$IMPORT_i$ and $EXPORT_i$ = import and export intensity, obtained from the DTI via the MICRODATA database compiled at the OECD. These data are virtually the same as were available in the Business Monitor.

$SFIRM_i$ = relative number of firms with no more than ninety-nine employees, from the Census of Production. One or two missing observations were filled using order averages.

$SIZE_i$ and $KAYO_i$ = log of industry assets and the capital stock–output ratio, obtained from calculations made by *D*. Allard for the Office of Fair Trading.

$UNION_i$ = per cent of workers covered by a collective agreement, from the New Earnings Survey. One or two missing observations were filled using order averages.

All other variables used were derived from these or directly obtained from the Census of Production; all market shares have been adjusted for imports and exports.

5 Entry and the Rate of Innovation*

1. *Introduction*

It is often said that competition is a dynamic process, and that it is the dynamics of the process which have a major effect on market performance. Our goal in this chapter is to explore the spirit of this suggestion by examining the association between innovative activity and one observable manifestation of competitive market dynamics, namely entry.

There are a number of reasons why entry—and small-firm activity more generally—is worth focusing on in connection with innovative activity. Chief amongst these is the recent policy interest that has been lavished on small firms in the name of rejuvenating industry and stimulating progressiveness. As is usual in these cases, elevating small firms up towards the top of the policy agenda has stimulated both a modest flow of careful research and a veritable flood of hyperbole. Numerous popular discussions have painted alluring pictures of a new industrial renaissance flowering from the seedbed of small-firm activity, and the same five or six anecdotal case-studies are regularly paraded in front of the argument by way of support. More scholarly examinations of the evidence have uncovered systematic evidence that loosely supports the spirit of some of these popular discussions. Small firms and entrants appear to make a fairly substantive contribution to the generation and diffusion of innovations, a contribution sufficiently large to dent the notion that there is necessarily a positive relationship

* First published in, and reprinted with the permission of, *Economics of Innovation and New Technology*, 1 (1991): 203–14. The data were obtained from the ESRC Data Archive at Essex University and from the Business Statistics Office in Newport, and financial support was given by the ESRC and the Centre for Business Strategy. I am obliged to Saadet Toker for useful comments and research assistance throughout, to Tassos Vlassopoulos for help with some of the calculations, and to Jonathan Haskel, Hiroyuki Odagiri, Steve Klepper, two referees, and the Editor for comments on an earlier draft. The usual disclaimer applies however.

between large firm-size or market power on the one hand, and innovation on the other.[1]

Establishing that a correlation exists between entry or small-firm activity and innovation is, however, only half the story. No less interesting and important is the further question of whether that correlation exists because entry stimulates innovation, or because new innovations open up market opportunities that small firms are either particularly quick or are unusually well suited to exploit. The question is an important one for several reasons. At a practical policy level, it is important to know whether aid given to encourage new business formation is feeding the causes or the consequences of innovative activity, whether support for small business is a (partial) substitute for or a (partial) complement to science and technology policy.

More broadly, it is interesting to ask whether market structure determines the evolution of technology, or whether technological trajectories shape the structure of markets in systematic ways over time. Although most economists have been mainly interested in the causal links running from market structure to innovation, there are signs that the causal channel from technology to market structure is no less important. Blair (1972) for example, has argued that many of the innovations introduced in the twentieth century have been deconcentrating, and there is some evidence to suggest that innovative activity has had a modest negative effect on levels of industry concentration (e.g. see Geroski and Pomroy (1990, reprinted as Chapter 3 in this volume), and references cited therein). The question is of both practical and policy interest, not least because it may help to clarify whether the increasing concentration of markets is a response to some relentless technological imperative, or just an expression of managerial ambitions.

The plan of operation, then, is as follows. In Section 2, we develop a model of entry and innovation that is general enough to describe both of the possible causal channels that may exist between the two variables. The model is applied to data on entry and innovation rates in the UK, 1974–9, and the results of the causality tests are reported in Section 3. Our conclusions are contained in Section 4.

[1] See Gort and Klepper (1982), Gort and Kanakayama (1982), Cohen *et al.* (1987), Geroski (1990, repr. as Ch. 4 in this volume), Beesley and Hamilton (1984), Pavitt *et al.* (1987), Acs and Audretsch (1987, 1988), and, for surveys of the empirical literature on the Schumpeterian hypothesis, Scherer (1980, ch. 15), Kamien and Schwartz (1982), and Baldwin and Scott (1987).

2. A Dynamic Model of Entry and Innovation

The immediate determinants of both entry and innovation, the 'condition of entry' and the 'condition of innovation' respectively, are a mix of permanent and transitory factors specific to each industry. The permanent factors are barriers to entry and technological opportunity respectively, while current market conditions register more transitory effects on entry and innovation.

Barriers to entry are structural factors that determine the ability of entrants to enter and compete successfully with incumbents, factors that include economies of scale, the degree of product differentiation, and absolute cost barriers (e.g. Bain, 1956). Barriers are said to exist whenever incumbent firms are able to maintain prices persistently above costs for long periods of time without attracting entry. Most discussions of barriers restrict attention to structural factors which, while being industry-specific, are also relatively constant over time and exogenous in the short and medium run. Barriers are not, however, the sole determinant of the condition of entry since the effect on entrants of a set of barriers of any given height or character depends on current market conditions and the strategic actions of incumbents. Economies of scale, for example, are a far less formidable barrier in growing markets than in shrinking ones, and their effect on entrants depends on the post-entry level of output that they expect incumbents to produce. Thus, while barriers to entry may be exogenous and constant in the short to medium run, the condition of entry—the specific problems faced by an entrant at any particular specific time—is likely to be only partially so.

Technological opportunity is the term usually used to describe the conditions that determine the number and kinds of inventions and innovations that it is feasible to produce given the existing knowledge base (e.g. Rosenberg, 1974). These conditions are exogenous to the decisions of firms, and they change only relatively slowly over time. However, while technological opportunity is the deep causal determinant of innovation, current market conditions and the strategic decisions of firms help to determine the precise timing of when innovations are actually introduced. Any particular technical breakthrough must always be embodied in a product before it can be offered to the market, and this means that both the timing of its appearance and its specific character are likely to be influenced by the actions of rivals and by the state of consumer demand. As it is a combination of deep structural factors and current market events, the condition of innovation is likely to be both less stable and less completely exogenous than is technological opportunity.

The major difficulty with using these observations to construct an operational model of entry and innovation is that changes in the conditions of entry and innovation (much less changes in entry barriers or technological opportunity) are difficult to observe. This problem has forced empirical workers to resort to rather incomplete sets of proxy variables. Some aspects of the conditions of entry and innovation are often reflected in easy-to-observe variables, and these have typically been used as a springboard to make wider inferences about the role of entry barriers and technological opportunity on entry and innovation rates. The hazards of this type of procedure are well known, and they are potentially severe enough to make one interested in examining alternatives. The approach that we shall explore here is to move away from trying to measure exogenous variables of interest, and to focus exclusively on the endogenous market variables that can be observed, entry, and innovation rates.

The attraction of this course of action is that, in principle, such endogenous variables *fully* reflect the *complete* set of exogenous variables of interest. Indeed, they might usefully be thought of as the visible features—the observable indices—of changes in the deeper latent variables that constitute the conditions of entry and innovation in markets. Since it is not possible to directly observe the conditions of entry and innovation, it is not possible to measure the effects of either on entry and innovation. It is, however, possible to make some indirect inferences about these effects because unobserved changes in causes will be recorded in observed consequences. It follows, therefore, that one ought to be able to say something about the causal effects of the permanent and transitory components of the conditions of entry and innovation by looking at the causal relationships that exist between observable indices of them.

To make this argument more precise, it is useful to embody it in an explicit model.[2] Suppose that all the latent determinants

[2] What follows is known as a dynamic latent-factor model; see Geweke (1977) and reference cited therein. Applications of the model include Sargent and Sims (1977), Pakes (1985), Lach and Shankerman (1989), Sullivan (1988), Diebold and Nerlove (1989), and others. For a general discussion of the uses and interpretation of factor analysis and latent variables models, see Aigner *et al.* (1984) and Judge *et al.* (1980, ch. 13).

of entry and innovation can be summarized by two orthogonal factors (i.e. sequences of serially uncorrelated shocks), a_t and b_t. A fairly general representation of the effects that these factors have on entry and innovation rates might be written as

$$E_t = \sum_{\tau=0}^{\infty} \alpha_\tau a_{t-\tau} + \sum_{\tau=0}^{\infty} \lambda_\tau b_{t-\tau} \qquad (1a)$$

$$I_t = \sum_{\tau=0}^{\infty} \theta_\tau a_{t-\tau} + \sum_{\tau=0}^{\infty} \beta_\tau b_{t-\tau}, \qquad (1b)$$

where I_t denotes observed innovation rates and E_t denotes entry. With two factors and two observables, the model is under-identified and we normalize the units of measurement so that $\alpha_0 = \beta_0 = 1$ (λ_0 or θ_0 may also be set equal to zero without loss of generality). Since a_t and b_t are orthogonal, any correlation that is observed between entry and innovation rates is caused by non-zero values of the λ_τ and/or θ_τ. That is, if E_t and I_t are correlated, it can only be because the b_t have an effect on E_t, the a_t have an effect on I_t, or both.

The problem is that it is impossible to measure the $\lambda_{\tau y}$ and θ_τ directly (much less to test whether they differ from zero) because the a_t and b_t are not observable. E_t and I_t are, however, observable, and they can be used to make inferences about the α_τ, λ_τ, θ_τ, and β_τ. The basic insight is that E_t contains information on a_t (and a_{t-1}, a_{t-2}, ...), E_{t-1} on a_{t-1} (and a_{t-2}, a_{t-3}, ...), E_{t-2} on a_{t-2} (and a_{t-3}, a_{t-4}, ...), and so on. Each observable is, therefore, a signal of one or more of the unobservables. This relationship may be inverted to express a_t in terms of all of the values of E_t and I_t that it affects, and similarly with b_t. Substituting these relationships into (1) yields a reduced form expressed entirely in observables,

$$E_t = \sum_{\tau=1}^{\infty} \Psi_\tau E_{t-\tau} + \sum_{\tau=0}^{\infty} \eta_t I_{t-\tau} \qquad (2a)$$

$$I_t = \sum_{\tau=1}^{\infty} \xi_\tau I_{t-\tau} + \sum_{\tau=0}^{\infty} \phi_\tau E_{t-\tau}. \qquad (2b)$$

The reduced form parameters Ψ_τ, η_t, ξ_τ, and ϕ_τ bear a straightforward relationship to the structural parameters of interest, the α_τ, λ_τ, θ_τ, and β_τ. Tedious but straightforward calculations reveal that

$$\alpha_\tau = \sum_{\tau=1}^{t} \Psi_\tau \alpha_{t-\tau} + \sum_{\tau=0}^{t} \eta_\tau \theta_{t-\tau} \qquad (3)$$

$$\lambda_\tau = \sum_{\tau=1}^{t} \eta_\tau \beta_{t-\tau} + \sum_{\tau=1}^{t} \Psi_\tau \lambda_{t-\tau} \qquad (4)$$

$$\theta_\tau = \sum_{\tau=1}^{t} \phi_\tau \alpha_{t-\tau} + \sum_{\tau=0}^{t} \xi_\tau \theta_{t-\tau} \qquad (5)$$

$$\beta_\tau = \sum_{\tau=1}^{t} \xi_\tau \beta_{t-\tau} + \sum_{\tau=0}^{t} \phi_\tau \lambda_{t-\tau} \qquad (6)$$

and $\theta_0 = \phi_0$, $\lambda_0 = \eta_0$. Thus, using (2) as a regression model, one can generate estimates of the Ψ_τ, η_τ, ξ_τ, and ϕ_τ which can be used in conjunction with (3)–(6) to produce estimates of the α_τ, λ_τ, θ_τ, and β_τ in (1).

Our interest is in examining the causal links that exist between entry and innovative activity. Although the interpretation that one puts on unobservables is inevitably arbitrary, we shall nevertheless associate a_t with the 'condition of entry' and b_t with the 'condition of innovation'. Consider first the possibility that the conditions of entry do not have any effect on innovation; that is, that $\theta_\tau = 0$, $\tau \geq 0$. Equation (5) suggests that the $\theta_\tau = 0$ if and only if the $\phi_\tau = 0$, $\tau \geq 0$, since $\alpha_\tau \neq 0$. Hence, the hypothesis that the conditions of entry do not cause innovation corresponds to the restriction in (2) that the term $\Sigma \phi_\tau E_{t-\tau}$ be excludable.[3] Similarly, the hypothesis that the conditions of innovation have no effect on entry corresponds in (1) to the restriction that $\lambda_\tau = 0$, $\tau \geq 0$. Equation (4) shows that this will be the case if $\eta_\tau = 0$, $\tau \geq 0$, since $\beta_\tau \neq 0$. It follows that an appropriate test of the hypotheses that the condition of innovation has no effect on entry is whether one can accept the restriction that the terms $\Sigma \eta_\tau I_{t-\tau}$ can be excluded from (2). Notice that the acceptance of either of these restrictions converts (2) into a recursive system.

Although (2) is rich enough to enable one to test the hypotheses of interest, it is unduly restrictive in its current form. The one feature of both the condition of entry and the condition of innovation that is not reflected in (1) is the relative stability over time of entry barriers and technological opportunity. Although they are not directly observable, the effects of such permanent features of market structure can be measured using panel data. The key insight here is that any permanent component in, say, a_t will have an impact on E_t, E_{t+1}, and so on

---

[3] This is essentially a test of Granger causality (Granger, 1969) and, as such, is a test of whether the terms in $E_{t-\tau}$ add anything to the linear predictor of I_t that uses information only on its own history (i.e. the $I_{t-\tau}$). Note that one cannot make any inferences about simultaneous causality using (2).

that is the same in each t. Thus, the permanent component in a_t will give rise to a permanent component in E_t that can be isolated from its time-varying or transitory components using standard techniques. Much the same applies to the permanent component in b_t whose effect will register on I_t over and above the effects of any transitory components. It follows, then, that one may observe causal patterns between E_t and I_t which arise from transitory determinants that the two share in common, or because the permanent determinants of both E_t and I_t are similar.

The model that this last observation suggests is a simple generalization of (2), namely

$$E_{it} = \sum_{\tau=1}^{\infty} \Psi_\tau E_{it-\tau} + \sum_{\tau=0}^{\infty} \eta_\tau I_{t-\tau} + A_i + \mu_{it} \qquad (7a)$$

$$I_{it} = \sum_{\tau=1}^{\infty} \xi_\tau I_{it-\tau} + \sum_{\tau=0}^{\infty} \phi_\tau E_{it-\tau} + B_i + \gamma_{it}, \qquad (7b)$$

where $i = 1, \ldots, N$ indexes industries, and $t = 1, \ldots, T$ time-periods. A_i and B_i are industry-specific fixed effects assumed to be constant over time, and μ_{it} and γ_{it} are white-noise residuals.[4] In effect, both A_i and B_i will extract an index of the stable features of the condition of entry (e.g. entry barriers) and the condition of innovation (e.g. technological opportunity) from the data. By contrast, the factors a_t and b_t only record the effects of transitory market conditions. The parameters Ψ_τ, η_τ, ξ_τ, and ϕ_τ associated with them show the response of entry and innovation to systematic time-varying components of the conditions of entry and innovation, components that reflect the transitory, day-to-day ebb and flow of market events plus any time-variation in entry barriers or technological opportunity. Finally, the residuals μ_{it} and γ_{it} capture the impact of unpredictable, idiosyncratic factors on E_t and I_t.

3. Correlations and Causal Patterns

The two observables that we shall work with are innovation rates and entry measured in four different ways. Our measure

---

[4] It is possible to put A_i, B_i, μ_{it} directly into the structural model (1), in which case the fixed effects and residuals that emerge in the reduced form (7) will be linear functions of A_i, B_i, μ_{it}, and v_{it}, the α_τ, λ_τ, θ_τ, and β_τ. There seems to be little purpose in trying to unscramble estimates of these primal variables (or of their stochastic properties) from their manifestations in the reduced-form equations, although the reader is free to do so if s/he wishes.

of innovation is a count of the number of major, commercially successful innovations produced in industry i at a time t. As one might imagine, the data are highly skewed across industries, and, to transform them into something more nearly normally distributed, we have elected to work with I_t defined as the log of unity plus the innovation count. All of our measures of entry and exit rates were computed by comparing adjacent tabulations of Census of Production, looking for enterprises new to the register or no longer in it. For the time being, we shall work with a net entry measure based on market penetration, the total sales of entrants in t less those of exitors in t expressed as a percentage of the total sales in the market at t. There are, however, a range of measures of entry that one can compute from these data, and an important part of the exercise will be to establish the robustness of the results to alterations in the definition of entry.[5]

The sample that we shall work with contains seventy-nine three-digit MLH (Minimum List Heading) industries, and, in the regressions that follow, we have pooled two cross-sections— for 1978 and 1979—together. The need to estimate the fixed effects, A_i and B_i, in (7), dictates the pooling of at least two cross-sections, while the need to estimate potentially long distributed lags limits the pooling that can be done. As our entry data only go back to 1974, we have opted to pool the minimum number of cross-sections necessary to estimate the fixed effects.

Four broad features of the data are worth noting. The first is the rather modest impact (measured in terms of both sales and the number of new enterprises) that entrants make in most markets on average, and the fact that exit flows are typically larger than entry flows. Table 5.1 presents some basic descriptive statistics on the count of innovations and the four measures of entry which illustrate this clearly. There is, however, a considerable amount of interindustry variation in the data and the second feature to note is that, truncation aside, values of

---

[5] The entry and exit data were drawn from a special compilation made by the Business Statistics Office. Market shares were defined as a percentage of total domestic production less exports plus imports. The innovations count was based on the number of significant technically and commercially successful innovations produced in each industry derived from a major study (involving 400 experts) by SPRU, University of Sussex, of 4,378 major innovations in the UK, 1945–83; for details see Ch. 2 above. Explicit attempts were made by the SPRU team to overcome a natural tendency to concentrate on the innovations of large firms in constructing their survey, and, although it is extremely unlikely, this may have imported a slight tendency to exaggerate the contribution of smaller firms.

Table 5.1. Entry and innovation for 79 three-digit MLH industries in the UK

		Mean	Max.	Min.	Std. Dev.
Innovations	1979	1.316	26.0000	0.0000	3.688
Count	1978	0.975	9.0000	0.0000	1.948
Gross entry	1979	0.0145	0.0680	0.0000	0.0218
Penetration	1978	0.0186		0.1098	0.0170
Net entry	1979	−0.0053	0.0519	−0.1295	0.0211
Penetration	1978	−0.0098	0.0889	−0.0765	0.0285
Gross entry	1979	0.0205	0.1227	0.0000	0.0253
Rate	1978	0.0342	0.0959	0.0000	0.0190
Net entry	1979	−0.0084	0.0720	−0.1363	0.0291
Rate	1978	−0.0064	0.0875	−0.1042	0.0303

Note: Entry penetration is defined as sales by entrants (net or gross of exit) a percentage of domestic sales; entry rates are the number of entrants (net or gross of exit) as a percentage of the number of establishments in the industry.

entry are roughly normally distributed across industries, as is I_t, the log of unity plus the innovations count. Both gross entry measures and the innovations-count variable are truncated at zero however, and have 34 per cent (gross entry penetration and gross entry rate) and 67 per cent (innovations count) of their values on the limit.

Of course, cross-section variation is not the only variation worth noting in a panel data-set, and the third interesting feature of the data is that cross-section variation is not, in fact, the predominant source of the total variation in the data. An analysis of variance of the innovations data pooled over the period 1975–9 suggests that roughly 58 per cent of the total variation in the innovations-count data is 'between industry' variation. For the four entry measures shown in Table 5.1, the corresponding percentages are: 49, 23, 24, and 21 respectively. That there is a substantial degree of 'within industry' time-series variation in the data raises the further question of how systematic it is. The fourth interesting feature of the data is that variations in innovative activity across industries over time are rather stable, but that variations in entry across industries over time are not. Thus, the correlation between variations in innovation across industries in t and that in $t-1$, $t-2$, $t-3$, and $t-4$

was always about 0.700; that between net entry penetration in t and in $t-1, \ldots, t-4$ never exceeded 0.100.

Taken together, these four features of the data suggest the following characterization of entry and innovative activity. Interindustry differences in innovation are slightly more pronounced than variations over time in the innovative activities of particular industries, not least because some industries simply do not innovate while others do so consistently. Current and near-future innovating industries are relatively easy to spot on the basis of their near-past innovation records. Interindustry differences in entry, by contrast, are much less marked, and the substantial variation over time in the entry experience of any particular industry is relatively unsystematic and extremely difficult to predict. These observations, in turn, suggest that the condition of entry is likely to be very sensitive to a wide range of perhaps idiosyncratic market conditions. Entry barriers, the permanent and deep structural determinants of entry, seem likely to be less a deterrent to entry as a limitation on the post-entry market penetration of new firms and, perhaps, a main contributor to the relatively high exit rates observed in the data. The condition of innovation, by contrast, seems to be rather more stable, and the constraints on innovative activity imposed by technological opportunities seem to divide innovators from the rest fairly clearly.

Given the quite marked differences in the statistical properties of innovative activity and the various manifestations of entry, it seems rather unlikely that either of the two will prove to be a major causal determinant of the other. Partial correlations between values of either across industries in t and values of the other in $t, t-1, \ldots, t-4$ are all positive but modest in size, never exceeding 0.215. Of course, partial correlations are likely to understate the cumulative effect of one variable on the other, and, in any case, they give no information on causal orderings. It is necessary, therefore, to probe somewhat more deeply using a statistical vehicle like (7), and Table 5.2 shows OLS estimates of a general and restricted version of (7). Equation (i) shows the results of regressing I_t on its own history (plus industry and time-dummies), while (ii) is a more general version of (i) that includes entry. The five restrictions that transform (ii) into (i) are that the $\phi_\tau = 0$, $\tau = 0, \ldots, 5$. As can be seen, imposing these restrictions on (i) inflates the sum of squared residuals by about 9.3 per cent. Applying a likelihood ratio test, the calculated $\chi^2(5)$ statistic is 14.1792, well above conventional

Table 5.2. OLS estimates of (7)

Dependent variables	(i) I_t	(ii) I_t	(iii) E_t	(iv) E_t
I_t	—	—	—	−0.0111 (2.745)
I_{t-1}	−1.066 (8.30)	−1.062 (8.48)	—	−0.0132 (1.870)
I_{t-2}	−0.7116 (4.96)	−0.6142 (4.96)	—	0.0095 (1.590)
I_{t-3}	−0.1554 (1.160)	−0.0943 (0.8241)	—	−0.0017 (0.2832)
I_{t-4}	0.1814 (1.262)	0.1933 (1.334)	—	0.0004 (0.0590)
E_t	—	−3.842 (3.089)	—	—
E_{t-1}	—	−2.440 (1.509)	−0.7367 (12.70)	−0.7348 (13.19)
E_{t-2}	—	−1.736 (1.097)	−0.6257 (6.146)	−0.6145 (6.223)
E_{t-3}	—	−2.493 (1.174)	−0.2587 (2.484)	−0.2767 (2.668)
E_{t-4}	—	−2.336 (3.129)	−0.0491 (1.608)	−0.0709 (2.220)
$\bar{R}^2$	0.7969	0.800	0.4850	0.4723
logL'H	13.56	20.65	478.348	481.951
SSR	7.7914	7.1227	0.02170	0.02073

Notes: All equations include seventy-nine industry-specific industry dummies and one time dummy, and all estimates are heteroscedastic-consistent. $I_t \equiv$ log of unity plus the count of innovations and $E_t \equiv$ net entry penetration. All estimates are heteroscedastic-consistent.

5 per cent significance levels. Together, the two calculations suggest that it would be imprudent to accept the restrictions $\phi_\tau = 0$, however modest the estimated impact of the $E_{t-\tau}$ is. Equation (iii) shows the results of regressing E_t on its own history, and is a restriction of the more general model (iv) that corresponds to imposing $\eta_\tau = 0$, $\tau = 0, \ldots, 5$. These restrictions inflate the sum of squared residuals by a modest 4.6 per cent, and the calculated $\chi^2(5)$ statistic is 7.206, well below conventional

5 per cent significance levels. It follows that the restrictions η_τ = 0 are not very costly. That the restrictions η_τ = 0 are acceptable but ϕ_τ = 0 are not suggests that the fully interdependent two-equation model (7) can be simplified to a recursive model in which E_t has an effect on I_t but I_t has no effect on E_t. That is, if one focuses only on the transitory determinants of entry and innovation, it appears that entry causes innovation, but that innovation does not cause entry.[6]

It turns out that this causal ordering is an extremely robust property of the data. Equations (i)–(iv) were replicated using all four of the measures of entry displayed in Table 5.1, and then, for each of the four entry measures, equations (i)–(iv) were rerun first with I_t defined as the count of innovations, then with E_t defined as the log of unity plus the entry measure, and then with both transformations. In eleven of the twelve cases, the results suggested that entry caused innovation but that innovation did not cause entry (using the levels of innovation counts and the level gross entry penetration suggested that no causal relations existed between I_t and E_t). The results also turn out to be robust to the estimation technique used. Repeating the exercises just described above using a probit estimator for the innovation equation continued to suggest that entry caused innovation, but not the reverse. Using a probit estimator for the two gross entry variables did, however, occasionally turn up weak evidence consistent with the hypothesis that innovation caused entry. We also experimented with subsamples defined by values of various exogenous variables. The most interesting partition divided industries into 'low' and 'high' concentration classes (defined by whether industry concentration was above or below the median concentration level in the sample), and tests suggested that the result that entry causes innovation could be observed only in high concentration industries. No casual effects were apparent in the low concentration group.

Thus, an examination of the transitory determinants of entry and innovation suggests that there are no grounds at all for thinking that innovation causes entry, but that there is some basis for arguing that entry causes innovation. This conclusion

---

[6] These exercises were also repeated without including E_t in the I_t equation or I_t in the E_t equation in the general specification, but this had very little effect on the results. Note that the causality test should not include contemporaneous values of the putative causal variable on the right-hand side, since it would enter regardless of causality if the two variables were correlated (i.e. the model permits no inferences to be made about simultaneous causality).

is, however, a little too simple and cannot be allowed to stand in an unqualified form. Both entry and innovation rates are also driven by relatively permanent features of market structure—technological opportunity and entry barriers. These two sets of factors are captured in (7) by the fixed effects, A_i and B_i, and the correlation that arises between innovation and entry through them is, in fact, strong and positive.[7] Estimates of the fixed effects retrieved from equations (ii) and (iii) in Table 5.2 were found to be correlated with coefficient 0.730. Regressing estimates of B_i on those of A_i yielded

$$\hat{B}_i = 0.7542 + 29.88\hat{A}_i + 244.08\hat{A}_i^2 \qquad (8)$$
$$(5.69) \quad (11.90) \quad (8.28)$$

with $R^2 = 0.71$, where t statistics are given in the brackets beneath the estimated coefficients.[8] The significance of the squared term in (8) suggests a particularly close link between sectors with very rich technological opportunities (high B_i) and those with very low barriers (high A_i).[9]

Thus, there are two sources of correlation between entry and innovation rates, and, as it happens, the two partially offset each other. The correlation that arises because the permanent determinants of each are similar is positive, and suggests that

[7] It is worth remarking that the fixed effects are estimated from two adjacent cross-sections, a very short time-period in which to get a fix on deep structural factors. Nevertheless, they play a substantial role in the estimated equations, affecting not only the degree of explanation achieved (suppressing them generally raised the sum of squared residuals by 200 per cent or more) but also the sign pattern on the lagged variables. Estimates of (7) without fixed effects generally produced positive coefficients on lagged dependent variables in both entry and innovation equations (although the negative cross-effects between entry and innovation shown in Table 5.2 were largely robust to this change). The negative signs on lagged dependent variables arise because the fixed effects allow each industry to adjust entry of innovation to its own long-run 'target'. Since this target is generally higher in high-entry or high-innovation industries, then both entry and innovation rates are in fact positively correlated over time.

[8] These estimates are heteroscedastic-consistent. Much the same outcome emerged using estimates of the fixed effects retrieved from (i) and (iii) and (ii) and (iv). The fixed effects from (ii) and (iii) had means and standard deviations of (0.9988, 1.756) and (−0.006, 0.0416) respectively. The mean of I_t, the log of unity plus the count of innovations, was 0.420 and 0.425 in 1979 and 1978 respectively. The system (7) was also estimated using the restriction (8) and allowing the μ_{it} and γ_{it} to be correlated, but the restrictions in (8) were much too strong to be data-acceptable. It is also the case that the fixed effects could not be simplified to a single constant in either equation.

[9] Steve Klepper has suggested (in private correspondence) that industries with greater technological opportunity provide more (and more varied) new, valuable information to potential and actual firms. If information cannot be (easily) sold, then new ideas that fall into the hands of potential entrants must be exploited via entry, leading to a higher entry rate in these sectors (*ceteris paribus*). That information flows facilitate innovative entry in sectors of rich technological opportunity is not inconsistent with the notion that entry barriers are lower in these sectors.

entry barriers and technological opportunities are highly related across industries. Industries that are rich in technological
opportunity appear to have lower entry barriers in general,
and, therefore, high levels of entry and innovation activity si-
multaneously occur in these sectors. Transitory determinants,
however, work the other way, and the correlation that arises
between innovation and entry through the lagged values of the
observables—a correlation that reflects the apparent causal
influences of entry on innovation—is negative. Using (3) and
the estimates in columns (ii) and (iii) in Table 5.2 to solve for
the structural parameters in (1) reveals that[10]

$$\lambda_0 = \ldots \lambda_4 = 0$$
$$\theta_0 = -3.842, \ \theta_1 = -2.202, \ \theta_2 = -1.2504,$$
$$\theta_3 = -1.1576, \ \theta_4 = -1.1065. \tag{9}$$

Thus, correcting for entry conditions and technological opportunities, increases in entry competition have a weak negative
effect on innovativeness.

In short, there appears to be a strong interdependence between deep structural features of markets (like entry conditions
and technological opportunity) that induces a positive correlation between entry and innovation, but that variations in entry
rates have a modest (and declining) negative effect on innovation rates. Table 5.3 reports some simulations designed to show
these two offsetting forces at work. Case 1 shows a simulation
of equations (ii) and (iii) from Table 5.2, setting $A_i = 0$, $B_i = 0.75$
for all i and $E_t = I_t = 0$, t = 1, $\ldots$, 4. Increasing A_i facilitates
entry, as shown in case 2 where A_i increases to 0.01, and, for
this reason, reduces the count of innovations through the transitory effects registered in (9). The reduction in innovation is
about 5 per cent in total over fifteen periods. However, (8)
suggests that A_i and B_i cannot be treated as independent parameters, and case 3 shows what happens when the increase in
A_i is mirrored in an increase in B_i by an amount given by (8).
Innovation rises considerably—by about 37 per cent relative to
case 1 and by about 45 per cent relative to case 2. Finally, were
B_i only to change, case 4 shows that innovation would be higher
still. As before, the negative offset from the effects described in
(9) lead to about a 5 per cent decrease in innovativeness.

It follows from all this, then, that there exists a positive

---

[10] It also emerges that $\alpha_0 = 1$, $\alpha_1 = 0.2652$, $\alpha_2 = 0.1022$, $\alpha_3 = 0.0739$, and $\alpha_4 0.0686$;
$\beta_1 = 1$, $\beta_2 = -0.062$, $\beta_2 = -0.0222$, $\beta_3 = -0.0201$, and $\beta_4 = 0.2398$.

Table 5.3. Simulations using (ii) and (iii)

t	Case 1		Case 2		Case 3		Case 4	
	E_t	I_t	E_t	I_t	E_t	I_t	E_t	I_t
1		0.00000	0.00000	0.00000	0.00000	0.00000		0.00000
2		0.00000	0.00000	0.00000	0.00000	0.00000		0.00000
3		0.00000	0.00000	0.00000	0.00000	0.00000		0.00000
4		0.00000	0.00000	0.00000	0.00000	0.00000		0.00000
5		0.75000	0.01000	0.71158	0.01000	1.03858		1.07700
6		−0.04650	0.00263	−0.04021	−0.00263	−0.06049		−0.06677
7		0.31848	0.00180	0.30573	0.00180	0.44459		0.45734
8		0.37086	0.00444	0.33305	0.00444	0.49475		0.53256
9		0.30129	0.00443	0.28070	0.00443	0.41207		0.43266
10		0.15321	0.00336	0.15965	0.00336	0.22645		0.22001
11		0.42069	0.00351	0.38348	0.00351	0.56690		0.60412
12		0.24862	0.00394	0.22731	0.00394	0.33555		0.35650
13		0.26039	0.00381	0.25282	0.00381	0.36635		0.37392
14		0.30422	0.00365	0.28366	0.00365	0.41630		0.43687
15		0.31768	0.00373	0.29143	0.00373	0.43002		0.45645
16		0.24080	0.00379	0.23002	0.00379	0.33500		0.34579
17		0.31211	0.00374	0.29288	0.00374	0.42985		0.44818
18		0.29298	0.00373	0.27096	0.00373	0.39870		0.42071
19		0.27747	0.00375	0.26094	0.00375	0.38191		0.39845
20		0.28458	0.00375	90.26778	0.00375	0.39186		0.40866
TOTAL	0.00000	4.8067	0.06406	4.5486	0.06406	6.60722	0.00000	6.9025

Notes: Case 1: $A = 0$, $B = 0.75$; Case 2: $A = 01$, $B = 0.75$; Case 3: $A = 0.01$, $B = 0.77$; Case 4: $A = 0$, $B = 1.077$. For Case 1 and Case 4 E_t is always 0.

association between entry and innovation that is driven by the positive correlation between entry barriers and technological opportunity, and, further, that the positive association is more than strong enough to overwhelm a negative causal effect running from entry to innovation that is driven by more transitory market conditions.

4. Conclusions

In this chapter, we have examined data on entry and innovative activities across a wide range of UK industries for the period of the late 1970s. The correlation between the two variables is positive, but, on the whole, rather modest, and it cannot be given a clear causal interpretation. Although there are noticeable negative effects running from entry to innovation (but none apparently that runs in the other direction), these are more than dwarfed by the strong positive correlation that appears to exist between the deep structural determinants of entry and innovation. The joint incidence of high entry rates and high innovation rates appears to arise because industries where barriers to entry are low are apparently also industries where technological opportunities are particularly rich.[11]

The reason for the weak correlation is easy to account for in purely statistical terms. Entry penetration and entry rates (gross and net) have a very high degree of within-industry variation, much of which appears to be rather unsystematic. Innovation rates, by contrast, have a more marked and more stable between-industry variation, and are more systematic in their variation both across industries and over time. The appropriate inference would seem to be that deep structural factors like technological opportunity play a much larger role in determining the condition of innovation than entry barriers do in determining the condition of entry. By contrast, current market conditions seem to play a larger role in determining entry rates than innovation rates, and the market conditions that matter for entry appear to be more idiosyncratic than those that matter for innovation.

[11] This observation is quite consistent with the results presented by Gort and Klepper (1982), who show that entry rates and innovation rates rise and fall together over the typical product life-cycle. It is also not inconsistent with the important role played by small firms in generating the new innovations recorded in our data; see Pavitt *et al.* (1987).

These results carry a fairly strong policy implication for those concerned to maximize the contribution that new small firms make to economic performance. In particular, a simultaneous rise in entry or small-firm activity and innovation rates probably should not be interpreted as necessarily suggesting that entry and small-firm formation are likely to cause a renaissance in industrial innovativeness. Rather, it may be no more than a signal that industrial rejuvenation is occurring for other reasons. Small-firm support schemes—however desirable they are on other grounds—may, in this reading of the data, do little more than stimulate a symptom of innovative activity rather than cause it.

6 Entry, Innovation, and Productivity Growth*

1. Introduction

It is widely believed that competition promotes efficiency, that a vigorous competitive process throws up alternatives in the form of new firms and new ideas, and that selection amongst them induces movements to, and movements of, the production frontier. Our goal in this chapter is to explore this presumption empirically, interpreting competition in a broad sense by taking the conceptualization new firms and new ideas literally, and examining the association between competition so defined and total factor productivity growth.

The plan of operation is as follows. The model that we shall use is briefly set out in Section 2, and is applied to UK data in the following two sections. Section 3 highlights some of the salient properties of the data, while Section 4 details the effects of competition that we observed. Our conclusions are summarized in Section 5.

2. Experimental Design: The Model

Total factor productivity growth is, by definition, the rate of growth of output less an appropriately weighted sum of the rates of growth in the various inputs used. The basic procedure for isolating that percentage of the increase in production not associated with increases in inputs is well known. Using any simple production function relating, say, labour and capital

* First published in, and reprinted with the permission of, the *Review of Economics and Statistics*, 71 (1989): 572–8. This work was supported by the ESRC and the Centre for Business Strategy. The data were obtained from the ESRC Data Archive, the Business Statistics Office, and from Steve Davies; Jim Fairburn and Saadet Toker provided excellent research assistance; and Mike Scherer, Bo Carlsson, Bruce Lyons, and two referees provided helpful comments. Needless to say, the usual disclaimer applies.

inputs, L and K, to output Y, one can express the rate of growth of output, y, in terms of the rates of growth of labour and capital, l and k, as

$$y = \alpha l + \beta k + \theta, \qquad (1)$$

where α and β are the output elasticities of labour and capital, and θ describes all other changes.

Our goal is to associate variations in θ with the degree of competition in markets. θ is usually identified by equating α and β with observed factor shares, but this procedure suffers from two potential drawbacks. First, if price differs from marginal cost, then factor shares in total revenue will differ from shares in total imputed revenue (marginal cost times output), and α (β) will not equal labour's (capital's) share in total revenue, but, rather, that quantity times the ratio of price to marginal cost (see Hall, 1988, and others). Second, inputs that are fixed in the short run will not necessarily be fully utilized all of the time, and, at a temporary equilibrium, their contribution will be valued at shadow prices defining factor shares which, in general, will differ from those defined in terms of observed market revenue (see Berndt and Fuss, 1986). For one or both of these reasons, then, the use of observed factor shares to measure α and β may give rise to systematic measurement errors. To avoid this type of problem, we propose to estimate (1) allowing the unobserved parameters to be industry and time-specific, modelling each in terms of observables.

Eliminating β through the assumption of constant returns, the regression programme can be written as

$$y_{it} - k_{it} = \alpha_{it} (l_{it} - k_{it}) + \theta_{it}, \qquad (2)$$
$$\alpha_{it} = \alpha X_{it} + \varepsilon_{it}, \qquad (3)$$

and

$$\theta_{it} = \theta Z_{it} + \mu_{it}, \qquad (4)$$

where X_{it} and Z_{it} are the observable determinants of α_{it} and θ_{it}, μ_{it} and ε_{it} are the unobservable determinants, and α and θ are the objects of estimation. The formulation (2)–(4) effectively allows each industry to have its own production function, and allows each industry-specific production function to shift at an industry-specific rate over time. To complete the specification of (2)–(4), it is necessary to be more explicit about the observables X_{it} and Z_{it}, and we shall consider each in turn.

Factor shares are widely thought to be roughly constant over at least the medium run, and there is evidence to suggest that this is also broadly true of the relationship between price and marginal cost (e.g. see Geroski and Toker, 1988, and references therein). This suggests that variations in the α_{it}'s can be parsimoniously described in short time-series by using industry-specific fixed effects. Introducing time dummies to capture any temporal variation induced, say, by economy-wide variations in capacity utilization, we write (3) as:

$$\alpha_{it} = \alpha_i + \alpha_t + \mu_{it}, \tag{5}$$

where the α_i and α_t are parameters to be estimated.

The θ_{it} are the objects of interest here, and our hypothesis is that increases in the intensity of competition will induce either (or both) movements to, or movements of, the production function. Previous work has used concentration indices as inverse measures of the degree of competition, but we wish to push beyond this and to explore other proxies. Most attractive in this context are proxies that reflect notions of competition as a dynamic process—as a flow of new firms and new ideas which result in new competitors and a rejuvenation of incumbents. The specific proxies that we shall use to capture this conceptualization are the annual market penetration by new domestic producers, E_{it}, annual net entry penetration by foreign producers, M_{it}, and an annual count of major innovations first introduced into each industry i at time t, I_{it}.[1] Since it is more than possible that the effects of any one of these factors will extend beyond the current period, we shall model θ_{it} as a function of the history of all three,

$$\theta_{it} = \theta_i + \theta_t + \theta^1(L)E_{it} + \theta^2(L)M_{it} + \theta^3(L)I_{it} + \varepsilon_{it}, \tag{6}$$

where we also have allowed for industry-specific fixed effects, θ_i, and time-varying effects common to all industries, θ_t, to capture the effects of other determinants of θ_{it} (see Caves and Davies, 1987, and references therein), and where the $\theta^i(L)$ are polynomials in the lag operator, L.

In an exercise like this, it is important to control for variations in all inputs (e.g. Jorgenson and Griliches, 1967), and, with output data based on the value of shipments, this requires

---

[1] Net foreign entry was used largely because gross foreign entry data are not available; it is defined as the change in import shares. We did experiment using domestic exit rates in addition to entry rates. The two variables are positively correlated with each other and with productivity growth, suggesting that the effects attributable to entry arise at least in part from displacement.

the inclusion of materials usage.[2] In this spirit, but with the intention of conserving degrees of freedom, we constructed an observed factor share-weighted sum of labour and materials per unit of capital (denoted f_{it}) to use in (2) instead of $(l_{it} - k_{it})$.[3] In fact, the only difference that emerged from using f_{it} rather than $(l_{it} - k_{it})$ is that the estimated effect of entry and innovation on total factor productivity was somewhat larger in the latter case. This is probably the result of cyclical effects not properly controlled for, and, to avoid the possibility of confounding cyclical and competitive effects, we shall focus on the results obtained when f_{it} was used.

These various decisions yield an empirical model

$$y_{it} - k_{it} = (\alpha_i + \alpha_t)f_{it} + \theta_i + \theta_t + \theta^1(L)E_{it} + \theta^2(L)M_{it} + \theta^3(L)I_{it} + n_{it}, \tag{7}$$

where n_{it} is a residual error which conflates ε_{it} and μ_{it}. For a sample of N industries observed over T years and using P lags in the three competitiveness variables, the model contains $2N + 2(T - 1) + 3P + 1$ parameters to estimate from NT observations, requiring that at least three cross-section panels be pooled.

3. *Experimental Design: The Sample*

The experience of productivity growth in the UK of the 1970s was unusual by post-war standards. At the aggregate level, the growth of labour productivity, steady but not spectacular prior to the 1970s, slumped in 1973, gradually recovered from 1975 onwards, and then slumped again at the end of 1979. Total factor-productivity growth was extremely low throughout, both absolutely and relative to the 1960s. In aggregate, output, labour demand, and, for that matter, labour utilization all slumped

---

[2] Bruno (1984) has argued that price rises of raw material will appear as autonomous technical regress, an effect that may even plague measures of productivity based on net output. Our view is that the time-dummies ought to capture the effects of such shocks satisfactorily, but including materials inputs seems a prudent course to follow.

[3] This procedure assumes that the output elasticities of labour, capital, and materials all differ from their observed factor shares by the same proportional amount. This will be true if the shadow prices of the three all bear the same relation to their market prices (i.e. if all three are utilized to the same degree), since the divergence of price from marginal cost affects all three factor shares to the same degree. Making this assumption effectively means that $(l_{it} - k_{it})$ can be replaced by an observed factor share-weighted sum of labour and materials per unit of capital, the coefficient on which will reflect divergences of price from marginal costs and shadow from market prices of inputs common to all factors of production.

in both 1973 and 1979, and this seems to have been the experience of the vast majority of individual industries.[4]

Our data cover seventy-nine three-digit industries for which we have information on materials usage, employment, real output, and real capital stock for the period 1970–9. The most striking feature of the data is their sheer variability. Output, inputs, and labour and capital productivity growth rates varied extensively across industries, each being roughly normally distributed with standard deviations three to ten times the size of their means. More interesting was the unusually high variation in these growth rates over time within industries: roughly 80 per cent of the total variation in these quantities was 'within-industry' variation year by year. Thus, while the distribution of growth rates year by year was roughly normal, the location of any particular industry on that distribution varied enormously over time. High productivity performance simply did not persist: rank and partial correlations of growth rates in labour and capital productivity across industries never exceeded 0.30 between any pair of years from 1970 to 1979.

Further, there appears to be evidence of structural change in the data. The mean output growth rate across industries varied enormously from 1971 to 1975, but then settled down from 1976 onwards at a fairly even level of 2.5–3.5 per cent. The mean growth rate of output per head (and per unit of capital) also stabilized post-1976 with, perhaps, some slight tightening in its distribution across industries. Although not decisive, these numbers do suggest the need for caution. We therefore ran a number of variants of the basic model (7) on samples constructed from all three, four, and five consecutive year pools of the individual year cross-sections, and conducted tests of structural stability on the parameters. These generated evidence of a structural break between 1975 and the years 1976–9, but no evidence of any breaks within the period 1976–9. As it is not obvious that the break in 1975 has anything to do with entry or innovation, the natural course of action is to pool the data for the period 1976–9.

4. Results

Equation (i) in Table 6.1 shows estimates of $\theta^1(L)$, $\theta^2(L)$ and $\theta^3(L)$ using (7). The effect of domestic entry and innovations is

[4] See Bruno and Sachs (1982), Mendis and Muellbauer (1984), Wenban-Smith (1981), and Kilpatrick and Naisbitt (1988).

Table 6.1. Estimates of (7)

	(i)	(ii)	(iii)	(iv)	(v)
E_{it}	0.0851 (0.5427)	0.4947 (0.4641)	0.8316 (0.7098)	−0.00691 (0.0078)	—
E_{it-1}	0.4202 (2.281)	0.4529 (1.669)	0.4910 (1.501)	0.4116 (1.678)	—
E_{it-2}	−0.2682 (2.616)	−0.2382 (2.352)	−0.2990 (2.93)	−0.2107 (2.0329)	—
M_{it}	−0.0411 (3.705)	−0.1141 (4.33)	—	−0.1209 (4.562)	−0.1178 (4.400)
M_{it-1}	−0.0312 (1.094)	−0.0183 (1.014)	—	−0.0077 (0.4411)	−0.0162 (0.9194)
M_{it-2}	0.0176 (1.277)	−0.0031 (0.3579)	—	0.0008 (0.0929)	−0.0015 (0.1785)
I_{it}	0.0030 (1.536)	0.0114 (2.195)	0.0169 (2.671)	—	0.0119 (2.323)
I_{it-1}	0.0024 (0.9184)	0.0071 (1.75)	0.0096 (2.242)	—	0.0649 (1.694)
I_{it-2}	0.0053 (1.824)	0.0062 (2.208)	0.0059 (2.105)	—	0.0053 (1.88)
R^2	0.8846	0.8917	0.8787	0.8875	0.8859
SSR	0.221172	0.207535	0.232328	0.215584	0.218546
LL'h	699.415	709.471	691.641	703.459	701.303

Notes: All estimated equations include 79 industry and 3 time-intercept dummies, and allow for 79 + 3 slope coefficients on f_{it}; NT = 316 observations. Equation (ii) uses instruments for E_{it}, M_{it}, and I_{it}, (iii) for E_{it} and I_{it}, (iv) for I_{it} and M_{it}, and (v) for M_{it} and I_{it}. The construction of these instruments is discussed in n. 5. Absolute values of t-statistics are given in brackets below the estimated parameters; all estimates are heteroscedastic-consistent (White, 1980).

positive, and that of foreign-based entry is negative; short- and long-run effects (the latter being the sum of the coefficients on current and lagged values of each variable) take the same sign in all three cases. The means of E_{it}, M_{it}, and I_{it} were 0.023022, 0.04592, and 1.21835 respectively, and thus it follows that the total effect on productivity growth of our innovation-count variable is by far the largest (in absolute value) of the three (in the short and long run). Further, the effects of domestic entry are (in absolute value) far more substantial than those associated with foreign-based entry. Only three of the nine coefficients have *t*-values in excess of 2, but this almost certainly exaggerates the imprecision of the estimates. The members of each of the three sets of independent variables in Table 6.1 are fairly highly collinear, suggesting that it is more reasonable to assess their collective impact on productivity than their individual impact.

Imposing the restriction $\theta^1(L) = \theta^2(L) = \theta^3(L) = 0$ on (7) increased the sum of squared residuals by about 18.6 per cent. The $x^2(9)$ statistic on these restrictions was more than three times its critical level, indicating that entry and innovations made a significant joint contribution to the overall explanation of output per unit capital. However, the fixed effects and time-dummies also added considerably to the overall explanation. Excluding the time-dummies for both slope (the α_t) and intercept (θ_t) lowered the sum of squared residuals by about 10 per cent. The calculated $x^2(3)$ statistic on their exclusion was four times its critical level. Eliminating the industry-specific slope dummies (the α_i) raised the sum of squared residuals by nearly 50 per cent, and the calculated $x^2(79)$ statistic exceeded its critical level by more than a factor of four. Finally, excluding of the industry-specific intercept dummies (the θ_i) raised the sum of squared residuals by nearly 27 per cent, the calculated $x^2(79)$ statistic being about twice its critical level.

The estimated effects of entry are fairly robust to a variety of respecifications. As noted above, they emerge when $(k_{it} - l_{it})$ is used instead of f_{it}, and their signs and broad magnitudes are not much affected by the assumption that production functions differ industry by industry and over time. Much the same results emerged when (2) was written with $(y_{it} - l_{it})$ as the dependent variable and $(k_{it} - l_{it})$ put on the right-hand side. Further, the effects are also observable when current values of entry and innovation are allowed to be endogenous. Equation (ii) in Table 4.1 uses instruments for E_{it}, M_{it}, and I_{it}, and produces results which suggest that simultaneity bias, if it exists, appears to operate in a way which minimizes the estimated impact of entry and innovation.[5] Equations (iii)–(v) drop each variable in turn and show, broadly speaking, that the effects attributed

[5] The instruments were generated from reduced-form regressions of E_{it}, M_{it}, and I_{it} on industry-specific and time effects, domestic entry, domestic exit, industry concentration, the level of import penetration, and innovation, all lagged up to six times. The broad features of the estimates in (ii) in Table 6.1 were insensitive to alterations in this set of exogenous variables; the validity of these instruments requires the absence of serial correlation in the entry and innovations data.

to any of the three variables in (ii) are robust to inclusion of the other two, and that none can be excluded from (ii). More interesting than the separate effects of each of the three variables is the set of effects each apparently generates over time. The effect of innovations is more or less constant over the three years, and, summing the coefficients in (ii), it appears that the ultimate impact of one more innovation on total factor productivity is (at least) twice its initial impact. By contrast, the effects associated with the two entry variables in (ii) diminish over time: the ultimate effect of domestic entry is perhaps 50 per cent larger than its initial impact, while that of foreign entry is perhaps 15 per cent larger in absolute magnitude.[6]

The basic message that emerges is that domestic entry and innovation have the expected positive effect on productivity growth, but that foreign-based entry has a negative effect. There are perhaps three explanations for the latter. First, given total demand, an increase in import penetration displaces domestic production without, however, reducing domestic capital stock, thus lowering $(y_{it} - k_{it})$. Second, it is often the case in the UK (e.g. in kitchen furniture manufacturing, as discussed by Steedman and Wagner, 1987) that high-quality foreign imports displace high-quality domestic goods, forcing domestic producers down market. Whenever this causes domestic firms to specialize in lower value added goods, one will observe a diminution in productivity growth during the displacement process. Finally, it is possible that the causation is reversed, that low productivity sectors attract a growing volume of imports.

Table 6.2 presents descriptive statistics on the estimated values of θ_{it} derived from (6) using the estimates from (ii) on Table 6.1. Those using (i) were quite similar, suggesting that estimates of θ_{it} are fairly robust to alternative assumptions about endogeneity. Movements in the estimated θ_{it} are broadly consistent with those of aggregate total factor-productivity growth estimates for this period, and with simple industry-specific productivity measures like the growth in output per head or per unit of capital. The latter are, however, much more variable than the estimates of the θ_{it}, and there are three senses in

---

[6] If it has any effect in Table 6.1, truncation bias (e.g. see Griliches and Pakes, 1984) is likely to affect the estimates of the effect of domestic entry, since the effects associated with innovation and foreign entry appear robust to the inclusion of extra lagged terms (up to five). Data limitations make only two lagged domestic-entry variables available, and this bias may account for the puzzling (but robust) negative effect of E_{it-2}.

Table 6.2. Estimated values of θ_{it} from (6) using (ii)

	Mean	Std. Dev	Minimum	Maximum
1976	0.0023	0.0248	−0.0076	0.0759
1977	−0.0128	0.0210	−0.0564	0.0533
1978	0.0197	0.0217	−0.0423	0.1191
1979	0.0075	0.0349	−0.1748	0.0997

Note: Mean and Std. Dev are the mean and standard deviation of θ_{it} across industries i for each t; Minimum and Maximum give the cross-section range for each t.

which this is true. First, the simple productivity measures have a much higher standard deviation and range across industries. Second, about 50 per cent of the variation in θ_{it} is between-industry variation, much higher than for the simple measures. Third, the variation in θ_{it} across industries over time is more stable than it was for the simple productivity measures (the correlation between θ_{it} across industries was generally in the 0.5 to 0.73 range for adjacent years). Like the simple productivity measures, total factor productivity appears to be roughly normally distributed across industries. For the period as a whole, the estimates from column (ii) suggest that the contribution of domestic entry to productivity growth is 0.0163 percentage points (computed as the sum of the coefficients, 0.7094, times the mean of E_{it}, 0.023). For foreign entry, the figure is −0.0062, and for innovation it is 0.0301. Clearly, innovation plays the major role in stimulating productivity growth and, in its absence, no growth would have been observed on average. More modestly but still of importance, domestic entry on average accounts for about 30 per cent of the effects on productivity growth attributed to innovation and both types of entry. Foreign-based entry has little apparent effect on estimated productivity growth.

Although it is not of major interest, the other output yielded by (i) and (ii) is estimates of α_{it}. These turn out to be very similar between the two estimated equations. On average across industries and years, $\alpha_{it} \approx 1.11$, and almost all of its variation is cross-sectional in nature. If one assumes that all factors are fully utilized, then these estimates of α_{it} suggest a mark-up of prices over marginal costs of about 11 per cent, slightly less than the 17 per cent estimate one gets from standard Census sources (e.g. see Geroski and Toker, 1988). We also included variables like industry concentration, entry, import penetration, innovations, and industry growth in (7) as possible determinants of α_{it}, but only the last was ever significant (it had a positive effect). Including, say, entry as a determinant of both α_{it} and θ_{it} made it difficult to sort out its separate effects on each, but, in general, most of the observables could be restricted out of the explanation of α_{it}, given that they were included as determinants of θ_{it}. Unsurprisingly, α_{it} and θ_{it} were mildly positively correlated across industries.

The effects of innovation that we have observed are not dissimilar to those that have been found using R. & D. or patents data (see the last five papers in Griliches, 1984), but the import effects observed here differ from previous results associated with international trade intensity. As it happens, using trade intensity rather than foreign entry in (7) tended to give positive coefficients that were generally significant, but more modest in size than those associated with domestic entry flows. Adding industry concentration to (7) produced a positive and often significant coefficient without, however, much affecting estimates of θ^1, θ^2, and θ^3.[7] These two findings make it clear that there remains a slight puzzle with these results, but this puzzle may have more to do with what one means by competition than with the effects that one thinks it might have on productivity growth. Further, although one can observe significant effects on productivity associated with industry concentration and import intensity, the contribution they make is largely picked up by θ_i in their absence, and these variables do not help to account for what is perhaps the most striking feature of the data—the large year-to-year variation in productivity growth observed for each industry taken alone. High import intensity and, even more strikingly, industry concentration are (relatively) permanent features of industries; high entry rates, innovation rates, and productivity growth are not.

---

[7] This is consistent with Greer and Rhoades (1976), and other work discussed in Scherer (1980). If concentration is linked to innovation, this may offset any static efficiency-reducing effects that it has, leaving a net positive effect on productivity. Scherer (1983) observed that the effect of concentration on labour productivity disappeared when R. & D. expenditures were included, an effect not present in our data, possibly because when variations in 'technological opportunity' are taken account of, the positive relation between concentration and innovation disappears; see Geroski (1990), rep. as Ch. 4 in this volume.

5. Conclusions

Our goal in this chapter has been to explore the effects of competition—new firms and new ideas—on productivity growth rates. Although entry and innovation rates do not fully capture the ebb and flow of the competitive challenges that incumbents must deal with, they do at least convey some of the flavour of change and development that occurs in markets. Industries which experience rapid changes in technology or host numerous new faces, year in and year out, are likely to be those in which incumbents are under some pressure to perform well. This rather uncontroversial proposition finds strong support in our data. Competition plays a significant role in stimulating productivity, with both new firms and new ideas provoking movements to, and outward movements of, the production frontier which, the data suggest, would not have occurred in their absence. Of the two, innovations play the more substantial role, but observed domestic entry rates account for at least 30 per cent of observed total factor-productivity growth. As entry and the innovation process are undoubtedly intertwined, the effect of competition might best be measured as the joint effect of the two, in which case it is clearly substantial. What is more, there are at least two reasons to think that these results understate the effects of competition on productivity growth. First, our estimates measure only the effect of competition that is disembodied and fail to account for effects embodied in new capital that replaces older vintages. Further, entry and innovation rates do not measure the intensity of competition in an exhaustive way, and probably capture only a part of the effect one would want to attribute to competition. These points made, it should also be said that issues of aggregation, simultaneity of inputs, and the assumption of constant returns may limit the generality of our results. Possibly more important, the effects of entry and innovation are difficult to disentangle from cyclical effects. Perhaps this is as it should be. The precise mechanism by which Verdoorn's Law is supposed to operate have never been made clear, but it is not hard to believe that, at base, it is new firms and new ideas that do much of the heavy work.

Data Appendix

The real (gross) output data were those used by Wenban-Smith (1981). Employment data came from the Census of Production. Capital-stock data were taken from calculations made by Dick Allard for the Office of Fair Trading. Materials inputs were computed by subtracting net from gross input and dividing by the ratio of gross to real output (which defines an implicit price deflator). Domestic entry was measured as the market share of all new firms appearing in each annual Census (i.e. measured gross, not net, of exit), the calculations being made by the Business Statistics Office. Foreign entry is the change in import share each year, derived from figures in the *Business Monitor*. The innovations data were annual counts of major innovation derived from the series on major innovations constructed by SPRU at Sussex (discussed in Chapter 2 above) and provided on tape by the ESRC Data Archive at Essex University.

7 Innovation and the Sectoral Sources of UK Productivity Growth*

1. *Introduction*

Identifying the sources of productivity growth is a popular pastime that combines interesting intellectual challenges with pressing topicality. To the extent that innovation is the engine that drives increases in productivity, then many of the interesting questions about the sources of productivity growth are likely to centre on the generation and application of new information by agents in the economy. Identifying the sectoral origins of productivity-enhancing innovations raises several further questions. Some sectors are more innovative than others, and it is of interest to ask whether this translates into a rate of productivity growth in these sectors that is sufficiently high to account for much of the aggregate productivity-growth performance that one observes. More subtly, one might ask whether the innovations produced in these sectors also have a significant impact on productivity growth in other sectors. Such cross-industry effects might arise between innovative producing and using sectors for a variety of reasons, or they might arise from spillovers related to either innovation production or usage. Indeed, since the fruits of research are a public good whose discovery and subsequent use involves more than a small element of serendipity, productivity growth in any particular sec-

* First published in, and reprinted with the permission of, the *Economic Journal*, 101 (1991): 1438–51. I am obliged to Steve Davies and the ESRC Data Archive for help in obtaining the data, to the Centre for Business Strategy for research support, to Keith Pavitt, Mike Scherer, Mark Schankerman, John Scott, Jonathan Haskel, David Currie, John Kay, Paul Stoneman and to seminar participants at the LBS, the University of Warwick, UMIST, the 1990 EARIE meeting in Lisbon, and the Troisième Cycle Romand en Économie Politique in Champéry for useful discussions, to Saadet Toker for excellent research assistance, and to the Editor and two anonymous referees for helpful comments on an earlier draft. The usual disclaimer applies.

tor is likely to depend as much on flows of knowledge through-out the whole economy as it does on the generation of new knowledge in that particular sector alone.

Our goal in this chapter is to examine the effects of major innovations generated throughout the economy on total factor-productivity growth in specific sectors. To do this, we propose to identify the main innovation-source sectors and assess the time-path of impact that their innovations have on productivity growth in user sectors, and in sectors that might benefit from spillovers arising from either the production or the usage of innovations. The main body of the chapter has two sections. The first briefly outlines the basic model and describes the data that we have used, and the second reports the results obtained by applying the model to data on UK productivity growth in the late 1970s. The final section contains a few brief conclusions.

2. *The Model and Data*

The basic method of measuring total factor-productivity growth and associating it with variations in innovative activity is well known, and we shall follow conventional practices fairly closely (e.g. see the papers in Griliches, 1984; the particular econo-metric model used here is basically that of Geroski (1989), reprinted as Chapter 6 in this volume). To identify total factor-productivity growth in any industry i at time t, one needs to subtract an appropriately weighted sum of the rates of growth of inputs, $f_i(t)$, from the rate of growth of output, $q_i(t)$. If the production function exhibits constant returns to scale, then this relationship can be expressed equivalently in terms of in-puts per head, $fl_i(t)$, and output per head, $ql_i(t)$. Our basic pre-sumption is that total factor-productivity growth depends, *inter alia*, on the use or production of innovations, $I_i(t - \tau)$, over time $\tau = 0, \ldots, \infty$.

In converting these observations into an empirical model, one must, of course, correct for a wide range of other sector and time-specific factors which also affect productivity growth. In the interests of parsimony, we shall do this by using fixed-industry and time effects that allow production functions and disembodied productivity growth to vary across sectors and over time in at least a limited way. The result is a model of the form

$$ql_i(t) = \theta_i + \theta_t + (\alpha_i + \alpha_t)fl_i(t) + \Sigma\beta_\tau I_i(t - \tau) + \mu_i(t), \qquad (1)$$

where θ_i and α_i are the coefficients on a full set of industry dummies, θ_t and α_t are the coefficients on a set of time-dummies (for all but one year of the sample), and $\mu_i(t)$ is a white-noise residual. In practice, $fl_i(t)$ is measured as the factor share-weighted sum of the rate of growth of capital and materials per head. Since observed factor shares differ from output elasticities (which are the appropriate weights to use) whenever prices exceed marginal costs or when factors are underutilized, the parameters $(\alpha_i + \alpha_t)$ correct for time and industry variations in monopoly power or cyclical effects.[1] The estimate of total factor-productivity growth that emerges from (1) is $[\theta_i + \theta_t + \Sigma\beta_\tau I_i (t - \tau)]$, which allows for variations across sectors and over time above and beyond those captured by $I_i(t - \tau)$. Pooling a sample of N industries over T years enables us to estimate the $2(N + T - 1)$ coefficients on the various dummies in (1) together with the coefficients on all P lags of the innovation variable, $I_i(t - \tau)$.

The sample that we shall be concerned with covers seventy-nine three-digit industries in the United Kingdom from 1976 to 1979. The selection of this set of industries was limited by the availability of data on capital stock and innovations.[2] The time-period was chosen on the basis of two considerations. First, changes in the methods by which the Census classifies industries made it impossible to extend the sample beyond 1979. Second, extensive testing for structural stability (on a range of variants of (1)) revealed that no structural breaks were observable within the period 1976–79, but clear evidence of a break emerged between 1975 and 1976. These preliminary experiments with the data also revealed that it was impossible to simplify the model (1) by removing any of the various sets of fixed effects. Not only was there clear evidence to suggest the existence of significant variations across industries and over

[1] See Hall (1988) and Berndt and Fuss (1986) respectively. Since deviations of price from marginal cost will have the same effect on all factor shares in total revenue and since utilization rates across factors are likely to be highly correlated, it is not unreasonable to take the difference between output elasticities and observed factor shares to be common across factors, and that is what α reflects.

[2] The real output data (based on shipments) are from Wenban-Smith (1981); the employment and materials data (gross less net output divided by the ratio of gross to real output) are from the Census; the capital-stock data are based on calculations made by Dick Allard; and the innovations data are counts of major, commercially significant innovations derived from work done by the Science Policy Research Unit (SPRU) at the University of Sussex (see Ch. 2 above). It should be noted that the standards used to identify 'major' innovations probably differ across industries, a measurement error which may make some sectors appear more productive than others.

time in disembodied productivity growth, but, more strikingly, there was also very clear evidence in the data to suggest that production functions differed across industries and, to a lesser extent, over time (see also Geroski (1989), reprinted as Chapter 6 in this volume).

The innovations data are counts of major, commercially significant innovations introduced into various three-digit industries in the United Kingdom, 1945–83.[3] The data have been classified by both producing and (first) using sector, and its most striking feature is the extraordinarily large number of innovations that flow between sectors (see also Robson *et al.*, 1988, and Chapter 2 above). In a real sense, most of the innovations recorded in the data are process innovations, being new products used as inputs in the production of products in other sectors. The major using sectors include the Non-Manufacturing sector (138 innovations produced, 1,642 used), Food, Drink, and Tobacco (82 innovations produced, 105 used), Vehicles (226 produced, 263 used), Textiles (146 produced, 481 used), and Paper and Printing (55 produced, 165 used). Major producers are Machinery and Mechanical Engineering (which together produced 910 innovations but used only 81), Instrument Engineering (546 produced, 120 used), Electronics (792 produced, 394 used), and Chemicals (413 produced, 167 used). Even the most cursory glance at the data suggests the existence of two major 'hubs' of activity, Engineering (defined as Machinery and Mechanical Engineering, Instrument Engineering and Electronics) and Chemicals, and these will be the two producing sectors whose impact on user's productivity we shall measure.

2. Some Results

(a) Innovations produced and/or innovations used

The first empirical question to explore using (1) is whether it is the innovations that are produced in a sector or those that are used which matter most from the point of productivity

---

[3] The average number of innovations produced per industry per year in our sample was 1.3, with a maximum of 36. The average number of innovations used, on the other hand, was 0.70 with a maximum of 31, the difference arising because non-manufacturing, which was a major user of innovations, is not represented in our sample. Both innovations produced and innovations used showed a high degree of between-industry variation (58 per cent and 75 per cent respectively), at least partly because a number of industries never produced or used any innovations while others were consistently high producers or users.

Table 7.1. Baseline estimates of (1)

	(i) —	(ii) Innovations produced	(iii) Innovations used
$I(t)$	—	.00053 (.2108)	.0102 (2.230)
$I(t-1)$	—	.00276 (.7363)	.00362 (1.160)
$I(t-2)$	—	.00181 (.7951)	.01385 (4.302)
$I(t-3)$	—	.00644 (1.778)	.00750 (2.349)
$I(t-4)$	—	−.00077 (.2702)	.00710 (3.057)
$I(t-5)$	—	.00563 (1.232)	.01621 (2.943)
$I(t-6)$	—	−.00176 (.5103)	.00980 (1.969)
SSR	.253563	.240836	.224879
L'LH	677.821	685.958	696.789
$\bar{R}^2$	.6108	.6125	.6382

Notes: All three equations include 79 industry dummies, 3 time-dummies, 79 industry dummies interacted with $f_i(t)$ and 3 time-dummies interacted with $f_i(t)$. $f_i(t)$ is the observed factor share weighted average of the rate of growth of capital and materials per head. Absolute values of t-statistics are presented in the brackets below the estimated coefficients; all estimates heteroscedastic-consistent.

growth. Roughly speaking, this corresponds to the question of whether the source of gain from an innovation arises from the knowledge created as part of the process of generating the innovation (in which case the number of innovations produced will matter most), or whether it arises because the innovation is embodied in a specific product or process that is valuable (in which case it is innovations used that matters most). Table 7.1 shows three sets of estimates of equation (1). The first includes no innovation variables whatsoever, the second includes current and six lags of the number of innovations produced by each sector, and the third includes current and six lags of the number of innovations used in each sector. Relative to equation (i), one cannot reject either the inclusion of innovations produced (equation ii), innovations used (equation iii), or both (not shown). One can, however, reject innovations produced in an equation that includes both innovations used and innovations produced, but one cannot exclude innovations used from the more general model.[4] Further, the effects of the number of innovations used on productivity growth far exceeds that of the number of innovations produced. Concentrating on long-run effects, the sum of the coefficients on innovations produced is .0146, while that on innovations used is .0684, nearly 3.7 times larger. Much the same applies to the relative effects of innovations produced and innovations used on productivity growth in the short run. On average across the seventy-nine industries in our sample over the period 1976–9, the rate of growth of labour productivity was 3.05 per cent. Since each industry used 0.7 innovations per year on average, the short-run contribution of each innovation used to the growth of labour productivity was 0.7 per cent; an industry that had used 0.7 innovations in each year since 1963 would have recorded an increase in labour productivity of 4.79 per cent in 1979 in the absence of any other increases in producing.[5]

It should be stressed that ranking industries by innovations used and by innovations produced generates two quite different orderings. The partial correlation between innovations used and produced across industries in any year never exceeds .35, and is generally rather lower. While each series is highly correlated with its own lags (on the order of about .80), neither is noticeably correlated with lags of the other (the correlation coefficients are on the order of about .15). The relative statistical independence of the two series arises from a rather surprising feature of the data: relatively few of the innovations produced in most sectors are destined for own (first) use. Across all industries, roughly 30 per cent of innovations produced are actually (first) used in the producing sector, and, in Engineering, the fraction of own use drops to about 10 per cent (see

[4] The appropriate calculated statistic for comparing (ii) to (i) is $\chi^2(7) = 16.274$, for comparing (iii) to (i) it is $\chi^2(7) = 37.93$, for comparing (ii) to an equation including both innovations used and innovations produced it is $\chi^2(7) = 33.066$ and for comparing (iii) to the more general model it is $\chi^2(7) = 11.404$. 14.07 and 18.47 are the 5 per cent and 1 per cent critical values of the $\chi^2(7)$ statistic.

[5] Neither these results not those that follow are (qualitatively) sensitive to the use of, $fl_i(t)$, the observed factor-weighted rates of growth of capital and materials per head. Using of the rate of growth of capital per head $kl_i(t)$ produced very similar results throughout. Regressions of both $fl_i(t)$ and $kl_i(t)$ on the full set of innovations variables (plus industry and time-dummies) produced little in the way of significant correlations.

Robson *et al.*, 1988, and Chapter 2 above). It seems, then, that one can make a clear enough distinction in the data to conclude that although both appear to matter, the knowledge embodied in new products seems to have a rather more profound impact on productivity growth than the knowledge generated as part of the process of producing the innovations themselves.[6]

The relatively weak effects of innovations produced relative to innovations used recorded in Table 7.1 is in line with work reported by Sterlacchini (1989), who regressed estimates of average total factor-productivity growth in fifteen two-digit UK industries over various subsets of the period 1954–84 on innovations produced and on innovations used divided by net output. He found the latter to have a larger and slightly more precisely determined effect on productivity growth than the former. The weak effects observed in Table 7.1 are also not inconsistent with those which one might have expected from reading the literature on R. & D. and productivity growth. Scherer (1982) explored the relationship between productivity growth and R. & D. in the US., discovering that R. & D. expenditures allocated to industries of use ('imported' or 'embodied' R. & D.) are generally a more important determinant of productivity growth than R. & D. expenditures allocated by industry of origin ('own process' R. & D.). Griliches and Lichtenberg (1984) observed much the same, except that they found own-process R. & D. to be generally significant, and observed a declining efficiency associated with embodied R. & D. They suggested an errors-of-measurement interpretation of the strong correlations associated with embodied R. & D. that springs from the observation that output deflators of innovation-producing industries (and, therefore, input deflators in innovation-using industries) constructed by the Census statisticians may fail to accurately reflect changes in user value associated with innovations. Much the same consequences arise when producers fail to fully appropriate the benefits of their innovations in the price charged to users. While plausible, the incomplete appropriability argument cannot be read as suggesting that the

---

[6] The results reported in Geroski (1989), repr. as Chapter 6 in this volume, are based on the innovations-produced data. The correlations reported there are slightly larger than those shown in Table 1, mainly because the entry variables (used there but not here) are somewhat collinear with the innovations variables (see Geroski (1991*b*), repr. as Chapter 5 in this volume, for an exploration of the relation between entry and innovation).

correlation is, in any sense, spurious. Rather, the implication is that conditions of appropriability are incomplete in most sectors. It is also the case that the way our innovations data have been selected—they are technologically significant, commercially significant innovations—may rule out major, sector-specific innovations devised for own use and not, therefore, subject to market transactions. The bottom line, then, is that whilst the importance of knowledge embodied in new products appears to be clearly recorded in the data, there is some reason to think that our results may understate the importance of knowledge generated as part of the process of producing innovations.

(b) The effect of innovations over time

The regressions reported in Table 7.1 assume that the effect of innovations (produced or used) on productivity growth lasts no longer than six years. The innovations are dated by the year of first use, and six years seems to be a rather short time for intra-industry diffusion, learning, and so on to be exhausted. It therefore seems worth exploring the time-pattern of effects rather more thoroughly (although this is an inherently speculative exercise to undertake with a short panel of data). A variety of experiments failed to reveal any interesting correlations between innovations produced or used and productivity growth after sixteen years, and the first equation displayed in Table 7.2 shows estimates of (1) with current and sixteen lagged terms in innovations used (qualitatively similar patterns emerged with innovations produced). It turns out that the last five lags (from $t - 12$ to $t - 16$) in the regression can be excluded ($\chi^2(5) = 2.044$) and the five before that ($t - 7$ to $t - 11$) cannot be excluded ($\chi^2(5) = 15.486$).[7] Table 7.1 is, therefore, not a completely accurate representation of the data. Speaking broadly, each innovation used has an initial impact on productivity growth of about .010, it continues to affect productivity growth by between .010 and .012 per annum during the subsequent six years (the sizes of the observed effects during the first six years are significantly different from each other), and the effect falls off to a rather imprecisely estimated .003 or so per year after

---

[7] It is difficult to compare this lag distribution to that which has been estimated for the relationship between R. & D. and productivity growth. Griliches and Mairesse (1984) uncovered 'some tenuous evidence for a rather rapidly declining lag structure' (p. 373), and both that paper and Griliches and Lichtenberg (1984*b*) provide some grounds for thinking that the effect of R. & D. lasts at least as long as eight years. That type of observation is not inconsistent with what we observe here.

Table 7.2. Estimates of (1) by source sector

	(iv) Total innovations used	Innovations used from Engineering	(v) Innovations used from Chemicals	Innovations used from all others
$I(t)$	.0107 (2.330)	.01844 (2.528)	.01479 (.8875)	.02669 (3.111)
$I(t-1)$	.00483 (1.407)	.06639 (1.477)	.02821 (.9799)	.02286 (3.036)
$I(t-2)$	.01735 (4.547)	.02551 (5.028)	.03597 (.8828)	.02503 (3.630)
$I(t-3)$	.00954 (.691)	.02623 (3.377)	−.03155 (1.270)	.00653 (.6623)
$I(t-4)$	.01097 (2.777)	.01906 (2.070)	−.00024 (.0010)	.01714 (1.942)
$I(t-5)$	.01970 (3.787)	.02322 (2.823)	−.0350 (1.078)	−.00409 (.4354)
$I(t-6)$	.00836 (1.263)	.02474 (2.495)	−.0072 (.2631)	−.03723 (4.153)
$I(t-7)$	.00308 (.6676)	.01299 (1.501)	.00094 (.0671)	−.02126 (2.844)
$I(t-8)$	.00323 (.8740)	.01538 (2.560)	−.0478 (3.921)	−.01426 (1.765)
$I(t-9)$	−.00567 (2.032)	.00160 (.3117)	−.01761 (1.684)	−.02989 (2.853)
$I(t-10)$	.00051 (.1442)	.03295 (4.649)	−.01088 (.9896)	−.02967 (2.598)
$I(t-11)$	−.00120 (.2717)	.00185 (.3311)	−.04577 (2.095)	.01255 (1.101)
$I(t-12)$	−.00015 (.0254)	.01086 (1.546)	.00068 (.0291)	.00812 (.7365)
$I(t-13)$	.00269 (.5653)	−.01342 (1.752)	.04167 (2.901)	−.00206 (.2561)
$I(t-14)$	.00355 (.7995)	−.00458 (.5618)	.01066 (.7265)	−.00525 (.4824)
$I(t-15)$	.00422 (1.026)	−.00083 (.0950)	−.02089 (1.453)	.01543 (2.068)
$I(t-16)$	.00249 (.6631)	−.00242 (.4170)	.02280 (2.491)	.00471 (.6772)

Table 7.2. (Cont.)

	(iv) Total innovations used	Innovations used from Engineering	(v) Innovations used from Chemicals	Innovations used from all others
SSR	.214125		.145960	
LL'H	704.532		765.081	
$\overline{R}^2$	.6300		.6628	

Notes: All three equations include 79 industry dummies, time-dummies, 79 industry dummies interacted with $f_i(t)$ and 3 time-dummies interacted with $f_i(t)$. $f_i(t)$ is the observed factor share weighted average of the rate of growth of capital and materials per head. Absolute values of *t*-statistics are presented in the brackets below the estimated coefficients; all estimates heteroscedastic-consistent.

that, being present for perhaps another five to ten years.[8] From an initial impact of about .010, each innovation used ultimately contributes perhaps as much as .0817 over eleven years or .0945 over sixteen years to productivity growth, about ten times the size of its short-run effect on productivity growth.[9] Much the same effects were observed when we tried (in a very simple way) to correct for cyclical effects by including a lagged dependent variable (whose coefficient was estimated as −.14177, with *t*-statistic = 4.1581).

(c) The sectoral sources of innovations used

As we have seen, most of the innovations that are used in any particular sector were produced in some other sector, and generally the source is one of the three Engineering Orders or

---

[8] It is worth re-emphasizing that the panel that we are using only covers four years, and this is a somewhat speculative basis on which to base the estimation of a sixteen-year lag distribution. This said, productivity growth has an unusually high degree of within-industry variation, and this means that there is quite a lot of time-series variation in the data. To see how sensitive the estimates of the lag distribution are to pooling, we re-estimated the model using data from only three years, 1977–9 and 1976–8. Short- and long-run effects were .0104 and .0907, and .0198 and .0574 respectively. These calculations plus the imprecision with which the more distant lags have been estimated incline one to think that our estimates of long-run effects may be slightly too generous.

[9] Although very desirable, it is difficult to allow the impact of each innovation to be industry- or time-specific given the length of time that each impacts on productivity growth. However, simplifying (5) by assuming that the β_τ are all equal to each other (definitely not a statistically acceptable procedure) reduces these seventeen parameters to one. Allowing that parameter to vary across industries and over time using the eighty-two industry and time-dummies produces some gain in explanatory power, but it is modest relative to the loss from the original simplification.

Chemicals. Clearly, the type of technology that is likely to be embodied in the innovations originating from Engineering differs from that embodied in Chemicals innovations. It is possible that one or the other type of technology may take on something of the character of a public good within the using sector, enhancing productivity in a wider range of the activities in that sector than the innovation is itself applied to. Differences may also arise because Engineering is the source of many of the capital goods used in the economy, and so is a natural source of process innovations. Further, market structures differ rather noticeably between the two sectors, and, in particular, the role of small innovation-producing units is far more marked in Engineering than in Chemicals (e.g. see Pavitt *et al.*, 1987). Small innovation-producing Engineering firms may well be much more user-orientated than the large innovating units in Chemicals who are noticeably more prone to produce for their own use. They may also be rather less successful in appropriating the full value of the returns attributable to their innovations. It follows, then, that either because of the type of technology involved or because of the conditions under which production and sale occurs, innovations originating from the two sectors might have rather different effects on productivity growth in using sectors, and it is worth trying to assess the size of the different effects.

To explore these ideas, we decomposed the total number of innovations used in each sector into three classes: those produced in any one of the three Engineering orders, those produced in Chemicals, and those produced elsewhere. Substituting these three for the current and sixteen lagged values of the total count of innovations used in each sector displayed in equation (iv) in Table 7.2 generates an equation with fifty-one innovation variables (rather than the seventeen shown there). The results of estimating this equation is shown as equation (v) in Table 7.2. It is clear at a glance that the different source sectors produce innovations that have quite different effects on productivity growth in using sectors. In particular, Engineering innovations have a major impact on productivity growth, with a long-run effect of about .2580 over sixteen years. On average, each of the seventy-nine industries used .51 innovations produced by Engineering per year over the period 1976–9 (the appropriate figure for Chemicals was .057, and for others it was .222). The short-run contribution of each to increases in labour productivity averaged 0.94 per cent per year; an industry that used .51 innovations from Engineering in each year since 1963 would have recorded an increase in labour productivity of 13.2 per cent in 1979 in the absence of any other sources of change. The long-run effect attributed to Chemicals innovations is actually negative (it equals −.0610), as is that attributed to other innovations (it equals −.0005), and the sum of the effects across the three source sectors is .1965, rather higher than that estimated in equation (v) in Table 7.2. Part of this difference is undoubtedly due to sampling variation, and, if it is truly innovations produced in Engineering that are the main source of productivity growth in user industries, part of the difference is due to measurement errors arising from the use of total innovations used (as in (iv)) rather than innovations used which are sourced from Engineering (as in (v)). Although both Chemicals and other innovations appear to have very little long-run impact on productivity growth, both (especially the latter) have noticeably positive short-run effects and neither set of variables can be eliminated from the estimated equation. Further, the sixteen lagged variables of all three innovation variables cannot be simplified to a set of six lags ($\chi^2(30) = 111.22$), although the last five lags can be eliminated.[10] When (v) is estimated, allowing for only eleven lags in the innovations produced from the three sectors, the effects attributed to Engineering = .1729, those attributed to Chemicals = .0613, and those attributed to innovations produced from all other sources = .0189.

It is possible to push this line of investigation somewhat further, breaking the Engineering-sourced innovations into three: those sourced from Mechanical Engineering (Order VII), those sourced from Instrument Engineering (Order VIII), and those sourced from Electronics (Order IX). More or less however one estimates it, the results always suggest that Electronics innovations have the largest impact on user productivity and Mechanical Engineering innovations have the least impact. For example, including eleven lags in each of the three

---

[10] A paucity of suitable instruments has discouraged us from exploring possible simultaneity biases involving $I_i(t)$ in (1), but experiments reported in Geroski (1989), repr. as Chapter 6 in this volume, suggest that if such biases exist, they seem to lead one to underestimate the effect of innovation on productivity growth. We also distinguished between innovations produced and used by the innovating sector from those produced elsewhere, and observed the latter to have a rather larger effect on productivity growth than the former. Closer inspection of the data revealed that this was because the 'outside' innovations were predominantly sourced from the Engineering sector.

Engineering-sourced innovations plus Chemicals and others yields long-run effects of –.0804, .2009, .4240, –.0119, and .0399 respectively. Relative to an equation where the three Engineering orders are aggregated, the log of the likelihood in this equation rises from 745.475 to 781.292, while the sum of squared residuals drops from .165245 to 131727. One concludes that it is Electronics and Instrument Engineering innovations most of all that deliver the impact that Engineering innovations have on users, productivity.

(d) Spillovers

The results discussed thus far are consistent with the notion that there are major flows of knowledge which emanate mainly from the Engineering sector (but also partly from Chemicals) and spread throughout the economy, increasing productivity wherever the new products and processes that embody this knowledge are used. Such effects on productivity growth are, of course, made more apparent in the using sector by any problems of appropriability that producers of innovations in Engineering have *vis-à-vis* their users, problems that may be less severe for the larger-sized innovation producers in Chemicals and elsewhere. However, while significant flows of knowledge almost certainly occur between the producers and users of innovations, there is a second set of knowledge flows that may be of importance. Economists concerned with problems of generating new technology have long been concerned with the possibility that spillovers from one sector to another may undermine incentives to do R. & D. These knowledge flows are often thought to occur between 'neighbouring' sectors: they may arise either from the process of producing or of using innovations and they generally occur despite the best efforts of firms in the sectors that give rise to them. Unlike the producer-to-user flows that we have examined thus far, spillovers occur between producers or users of different innovations.

Spillovers are often modelled by examining cross-correlations between R. & D. done in one sector and productivity in a neighbouring sector. The analogous exercise using innovations data might run as follows. Equation (iv) in Table 7.3 includes current and sixteen lagged values of the total number of innovations used in each three-digit industry. Spillovers are most likely to occur between neighbours within two-digit industries (but see Scott and Pascoe, 1987: 195–7), so to this equation we add current and sixteen lagged variables reflecting the number of

Table 7.3. Estimates of (1) including spillovers

	(vi) Spillovers from innovations used elsewhere in same 2-digit industry	(vii) Spillovers from innovations produced elsewhere in same 2-digit industry	(viii) As in (vii) but only those sourced from Engineering
$S(t)$	−.00090 (.5251)	−.00226 (1.753)	−.00255 (1.133)
$S(t-1)$	.000182 (.1099)	−.00267 (2.028)	.00016 (.0827)
$S(t-2)$	−.00130 (.6509)	.00239 (1.297)	−.00279 (1.803)
$S(t-3)$	−.00466 (1.977)	−.00676 (1.782)	−.00350 (1.791)
$S(t-4)$	−.00283 (.9378)	−.00676 (3.833)	−.00110 (.3395)
$S(t-5)$	−.00267 (.8627)	−.00614 (3.155)	−.00019 (.3824)
$S(t-6)$	−.00171 (.5385)	−.00429 (1.821)	.00219 (.6191)
$S(t-7)$	.00311 (1.422)	.00082 (.3681)	.00893 (3.026)
$S(t-8)$	.00239 (1.081)	.00382 (2.671)	.00231 (.9881)
$S(t-9)$	.00127 (.5896)	.00131 (.8307)	.00433 (2.062)
$S(t-10)$	.00184 (.8767)	.00352 (2.531)	.00335 (1.084)
$S(t-11)$	−.00076 (.2715)	.00191 (1.142)	.00090 (.2266)
$S(t-12)$	−.00190 (.7613)	.00106 (.6756)	−.00207 (.4767)
$S(t-13)$	−.00216 (.7950)	−.00254 (1.906)	.00067 (.1290)
$S(t-14)$	.00332 (1.563)	.00194 (2.031)	.00150 (.2756)
$S(t-15)$	−.00266 (1.124)	.00249 (2.164)	−.00615 (1.009)
$S(t-16)$	−.00283 (1.281)	.00242 (1.654)	−.00386 (.8049)

Table 7.3. (Cont.)

	(vi) Spillovers from innovations used elsewhere in same 2-digit industry	(vii) Spillovers from innovations produced elsewhere in same 2-digit industry	(viii) As in (vii) but only those sourced from Engineering
SSR	.198368	.168385	.193103
LL'H	716.609	742.500	720.859
$\overline{R}^2$	.6078	.6671	.6182

Notes: In addition to current and 16 lags in the number of innovations used, all 3 equations include 79 industry dummies, 3 time-dummies, 79 industry dummies interacted with $f_i(t)$ and 3 time-dummies interacted with $f_i(t)$. $f_i(t)$ is the observed factor share weighted average of the rate of growth of capital and materials per head. Absolute values of t-statistics are presented in the brackets below the estimated coefficients; all estimates heteroscedastic-consistent.

innovations used and/or produced *elsewhere* in the two-digit industry in which each three-digit industry finds itself. Table 7.3 displays three such regressions in which the spillover variables are: the total number of innovations used *elsewhere* in the appropriate two-digit sector, the total number of innovations produced *elsewhere* in the two-digit sector, and the total number of innovations used *elsewhere* in the two-digit sector that originate from Engineering.[11] In all three cases, there appear to be fairly significant spillover effects, but they are always quite small in magnitude. The long-run effect of the total number of innovations used elsewhere in a particular two-digit sector is estimated to be −.0123 in equation (vi), the production of innovations elsewhere has a long-run effect estimated to be −.00062 in equation (vii), and the use elsewhere of innovations sourced from Engineering has a long-run effect estimated to be .00021 in equation (viii). Although the various spillover variables cannot be completely excluded ($\chi^2(17) = 24.154$, $\chi^2(17) = 75.936$, and $\chi^2(17) = 32.654$ respectively for equations (vi)–(viii) *vis-à-vis* (iv) in Table 2), they do not appear to represent a major intersectoral flow of knowledge.

That there appear to be very little in the way of spillovers in these data is mildly interesting in view of previous results that

[11] We also experimented by modelling spillovers as the total number of innovations used elsewhere in the appropriate two-digit industry that originated in Chemicals, as well as measures involving total economy-wide usage or production of the innovations. All these variables produced qualitatively similar results to those discussed in the text.

have appeared in the literature. Levin (1988), Levin and Reiss (1988), Bernstein and Nadiri (1988 and 1989), Jaffee (1986), and others report the existence of noticeable spillovers between neighbouring sectors (defined in different ways) in the effects of R. & D. spending on costs, patents, profits, and other measures of performance. That similar effects are not observed when measures of innovative output—such as innovation counts—are associated with productivity growth can be taken to suggest that what spills over between neighbouring sectors (defined as other activities within the same two-digit industry) is knowledge in general, not knowledge embodied in a specific product (which, presumably, is too user-specific to be of much immediate value to others). That is, knowledge embodied in new products seems to spill over between user and producer sectors, but not between neighbouring using sectors; neighbours seem to share a more general type of disembodied knowledge that is, apparently, more closely related to the process of producing (rather than using) innovations.

4. *Some Conclusions*

Our goal in this chapter has been to identify the major inter-industry flows of knowledge in the UK economy, and to assess their importance. This we have done by associating innovations used in particular sectors but produced elsewhere and innovations used and produced in neighbouring sectors with increases in productivity in particular innovation-using sectors. The three major empirical results that we have uncovered are: first, that innovations have a long-run effect (requiring perhaps as long as 10–15 years to realize) on productivity growth that may be as much as ten times the size of their short-run effect; second, that it is innovations used (and particularly those originating in Engineering) that have the biggest impact on productivity growth, not innovations produced; and third, that the size of spillovers from the production or use of innovations in neighbouring sectors is extremely modest. Thus, major flows of knowledge embodied in specific products seem to flow between producers and users of specific innovations (particularly those originating in Engineering), but knowledge that spills over between neighbouring users or producers of innovations is disembodied.

While these results suggest that innovations used account for much of observed total factor-productivity growth, there are two reasons to think that they may actually understate the true total effect of innovation on productivity growth: first, we have concentrated on measuring the effects of innovation on dis-embodied productivity growth, and have not identified those effects that are embodied in factor inputs; and, second, we have not traced the productivity effects of those innovations first used in non-manufacturing (nearly 25 per cent of the 1945–83 total). Set against these biases are two that might work in the other direction. Our estimates of very long lag distributions on short panels of data plus our use of sixteen lags to calculate long-run effects may well have exaggerated these. More impor-tant, the use of fixed and common time-effects undoubtedly fails to correct for idiosyncratic industry cyclical effects on productivity. To the extent that innovation production or use is pro-cyclical (not obviously evident in the data), this failure to account for cyclical effects may bias up estimates of the effects of innovation on productivity growth. Finally, while we have assessed the effects of the innovations in the SPRU data-set on productivity growth, one needs to be slightly cautious about generalizing these results to the effects of the use of *all* inno-vations on productivity growth. It is simply not clear whether the heavy users of innovations identified by SPRU also import other innovations not produced in the United Kingdom and use more minor innovations as intensively as they use major innovations (in which case, one might hazard a generaliza-tion), or not (in which case, our results are sample-specific).

Two final reflections seem to be in order. One rather obvious implication of these results relates to the use of innovation counts as measures of 'innovativeness'. In effect, what we have done here is to allow innovations produced in different sectors to record separate effects on users' productivity. These separate effects can be thought of as weights that can be used to value each type of innovation in terms of its 'quality'. Seen in this light, the results presented here can be read as suggesting that there is considerable heterogeneity even amongst the class of major, commercially significant innovations, and, therefore, that simple counts of innovations produced or used may be mis-leading. A second implication of these results follows from the observation that it is innovations used rather than innovations produced that have major effects on productivity growth. Broadly speaking, this suggests that it is the use as much (if not more) as it is the production of innovation that one ought to encourage as part of one's efforts to increase UK competitive-ness. In particular, the results are consistent with the view that industrial policies designed to stimulate the generation of new knowledge may prove to be much less effective than policies designed to stimulate the diffusion of existing knowledge. If, as one imagines, such policies are targeted at specific sectors, then our results suggest that the flows of knowledge emanating from Engineering might repay much closer examination.

8 The Profitability of Innovating Firms*

1. Introduction

The question of whether private rates of return are too low to encourage enough innovation by firms has been a perennial concern of UK industrial policy-makers, and numerous schemes have been (and continue to be) developed to help stimulate the generation and diffusion of innovations. In this chapter, we propose to cast some light on this problem by measuring the effect that the production of major innovations has on the profitability of innovation-producing firms (and their rivals).

Although the existence and size of the correlation between innovation and profitability is our main interest (and it is one that we share with a large and growing literature), we are also interested in asking two specific questions about that correlation. First, is the relationship between profits and innovative *output* (i.e. the production of major innovations) similar to that which has been found between profits and research *inputs* (i.e. R. & D. expenditures) or patent counts (which are typically more highly correlated with research inputs than with measures of innovative output)?[1] The question is important because the relationship between research inputs and different measures of innovative output is complex and poorly understood. Indeed,

* With Steve Machin and John Van Reenen; first published in, and reprinted with the permission of, the *Rand Journal of Economics*, 24 (1993): 198–211. We are obliged to the ESRC Data Archive for providing the innovations data-tape, to Saadet Toker for producing the data that we needed from it, and to the ESRC, the Centre for Business Strategy, the Institute for Fiscal Studies, and the Leverhulme Trust for research support. Participants at the ESRC Industrial Economics Study Group meeting at Cardiff in March 1991, and the 1991 EARIE Conference at Ferrara provided helpful comments, as did John Scott, Tim Bresnahan, Jonathan Haskel, Paul Stoneman, James Poterba, and an anonymous referee. The usual disclaimer applies.

[1] For work on the returns to R. & D. and/or to patenting activity, see Shankerman and Pakes (1986); Pakes (1986); Shankerman (1991); Cockburn and Griliches (1988); the papers in Griliches (1984); the survey in Griliches (1990); and others. Mansfield *et al.*, (1979); Bresnahan (1986); Trajtenberg (1989); and others look at the divergence between private and social rates of return.

there is much to be said in any case for focusing directly on the effects of new products and processes introduced into the market: after all, not all firms that introduce major innovations do R. & D., and most patents protect relatively minor innovations. Our main conclusion on this issue is that the use of innovative *output* measures generates quite different estimates of the size of spillovers than measures of innovative *input* measures do.

Our second question is: does the correlation between innovative output and profitability reflect transitory or permanent performance differences between innovating and non-innovating firms? This distinction is important because it corresponds to two quite different views about why innovation may be associated with superior performance: that it is the *product of the innovative process* which matters because new innovations favourably affect a firm's market position, and that it is the *process of innovation* which matters because it transforms a firm's internal capabilities. The first, and more commonly held, of these two views argues that the production of new products or processes strengthens a firm's competitive position *vis-à-vis* its rivals. As a consequence, its profits increase and remain high until rivals successfully imitate and begin to eat into the innovator's rents. An alternative and rather less common view asserts that the process of innovation transforms a firm, building up its core competencies in a variety of ways which make it quicker, more flexible, more adaptable, and more capable in dealing with market pressures than non-innovating firms. In this second view, innovation is itself often the consequence of a more fundamental transformation that occurs within an innovating firm. Evaluating the relative merits of these two views helps to make clear whether policies designed to stimulate innovation ought to concentrate on ameliorating discouraging features of the market environment in which product and process innovations are sold, or on strengthening the internal capabilities of firms.

At a statistical level, the difference between these two views of the effect of innovation turns on whether the returns to the production of innovations are transitory and associated with the production of a specific innovation (the *product view*), or on whether they are permanent and associated with generic differences between innovators and non-innovators (the *process view*). To explore these two views about the effect of innovation on profitability, then, one needs to examine whether the profit differences between innovating and non-innovating firms which we observe are attributable to specific innovations produced at specific times, to some other (transitory) observable difference, or to a permanent and relatively fixed difference in the profitability of the two types of firm. Our main conclusion on this issue is that large fixed differences in profitability exist between innovators and non-innovators, but that these differences are observable only in recessions. That is, innovating firms appear to differ generically from non-innovators in ways which make them less sensitive to cyclical downturns.

Our plan is as follows. In Section 2 below, we shall briefly set out the empirical model, discuss the variables to be used and outline the structure of testing. Our data base contains 721 UK manufacturing firms observed over the period 1972–83, of which 117 produced at least one innovation during that period. In Section 3, we present some estimates of the effects of innovations on price–cost margins and profits for the sample of 721 firms, discussing a number of further experiments designed to check the robustness of the conclusions and provide further information on the properties of the sample. Then, in Section 4, we focus on the sample of 117 innovating firms, looking for differences between them and the full population of 721 firms. Section 5 summarizes the main results of the analysis.

2. *The Experiment*

The basic empirical model that we use is designed to produce simple but robust measures of the effects of innovation on profitability. The main difficulty to be overcome is the formulation of a reasonably clean experimental setting in which to measure these effects, i.e. correcting for other factors that affect profitability, particularly those which might be associated with innovation. The literature suggests that innovation is likely to be affected by firm size, market structure, conditions of appropriability, the state of technological opportunity, and perhaps internal cash flow. Since many of these variables also affect profitability, we have built our empirical model up from conventional structure-performance foundations.[2] In particular, we model profit margins (*ROR*) as being determined by market

[2] For recent work on profitability that follows similar lines, see Kwoka and Ravenscraft (1986); Schmalensee (1987); Machin and van Reenen (1992); and others. Surveys of the empirical work on the effects of market structure, firm size, conditions of appropriability, and technological opportunity on R. & D., patenting, and innovation include Cohen and Levin (1989); Baldwin and Scott (1987); and Scherer and Ross (1990).

shares (*MS*), industry concentration (*CON*), import intensity (*IMP*), and the interaction between shares and concentration (*MS*CON*). Since rents attributable to market shares or concentration are often siphoned off by labour, we also include a measure of unionization (*UN*) as a determinant of margins. We also allow for time-dummies, for firm-specific fixed effects to correct for variations in technological opportunity and conditions of appropriability across firms, and for systematic time-varying effects associated with departures from and the subsequent return to equilibrium. Following Geroski and Jacquemin (1988) we capture these last effects using lagged margins (ROR_{t-1}).[3]

To capture the effects of innovation on profitability, we use two types of variables. Both are derived from a major study of innovations in the UK undertaken by SPRU at the University of Sussex. This project identified technologically important and commercially significant innovations produced in particular years (over the period 1945–83), locating both producers and users in specific three-digit (*MLH*) industries and tracking down the ownership of each innovating unit (see Chapter 2 for further details). The main variable of interest for our purposes here is the number of innovations produced by each innovating unit or firm in any year (*INN*), and we allow it to have effects on profitability for up to six years. The other two innovation variables that we shall use are designed to capture any spillovers that occur within two-digit industries, and they are the number of innovations produced (*IPI*) and the number of innovations used (*IUI*) elsewhere in the two-digit industry in which the firm operates.

Thus, using i subscripts to identify firms and t subscripts for time, our estimating equation is

$$ROR_{it} = f_i + \alpha_0{}^*MS_{it} + \alpha_1{}^*CON_{it} + \alpha_2{}^*IMP_{it} + \alpha_3{}^*(MS_{it}{}^*CON_{it})$$
$$+ \alpha_4{}^*UN_{it} + \alpha_5{}^*ROR_{it-1} + \alpha_6{}^*IPI_{it} + \alpha_7{}^*IUI_{it} + \alpha_8{}^*T_t$$
$$+ \sum_{j=0}^{6} \lambda_j INN_{it-j} + \mu_{it}, \qquad (1)$$

---

[3] One could interpret the lagged-margins term as reflecting cash-flow influences on innovative activity which feed through to innovation and thence to profitability within a year or so. Indeed, one might wish to endogenize the variables measuring current innovation rates to ensure that any contemporaneous feedback from profits to innovations does not create bias. However, we believe that cash flow is much more relevant to decisions about the level of research inputs a firm chooses than to the timing of innovative output, and we are sure that feedbacks between profits and innovative output operate with very long lags (if at all).

where f_i is a firm-specific fixed effect, T_t is a time-dummy common to all firms, and μ_{it} is assumed to be a normally distributed *iid* random variable. The short-run impact of innovation on margins is measured by λ_0; in the long run, each innovation has an effect on margins of $\sum_j \lambda_j / (1 - \alpha_5)$.

Table 8.1 provides a somewhat more precise description of the observables to be used in (1), together with estimates of the mean and standard deviation of each (over the period used in the estimation) for the sample of 721 firms (hereafter, 'the population'), and for the sample of 117 firms who innovated at least once during the period (hereafter, 'the innovators'). Both of these panels are unbalanced in that there are different numbers of observations per firm, mainly due to different dates of entry into the databank. The criterion for including a firm in our sample is that at least seven continuous time-series observations (out of a maximum of twelve) are available.[4]

In what follows, we shall (by and large) estimate (1) by differencing out the fixed effects, using an instrument for the lagged dependent variable (and, occasionally, some of the other variables). It is well known that in dynamic panel data models the usual transformations used to eliminate fixed effects (within-groups or first-differencing) induce bias in the estimated co-efficient on the lagged dependent variable (see Nickell, 1981). A number of instrumental variable techniques have been proposed to circumvent this problem. Anderson and Hsaio (1982), for example, propose the use of $(t - 2)$ dated levels or differences of the dependent variable as valid instruments for a $(t - 1)$ dated lagged dependent variable in a first-differenced panel data model. Amemiya and McCurdy (1986) recommend stacking the instruments by year so as to make available more instruments. We use a dynamic panel data estimator recently proposed by Arellano and Bond (1991) (see also Holtz-Eakin *et al.*, 1988) which makes full use of all possible orthogonality conditions to generate a more efficient estimator. The logic behind this estimator is quite straightforward, namely that the further advanced is the panel the more instruments are available for use. For

---

[4] These 721 companies are manufacturing companies taken from the Datastream databank, and they are large quoted companies. In 1979, the total sales of our sample is 55.3 per cent of total manufacturing sales as reported in the Census of Production. The exact balance of the panel is 10 firms with 7 records, 19 firms with 8, 40 firms with 9, 44 with 10, 69 with 11, and 539 with the maximum 12 time-series observations. We will report results using the balanced panel of 539 companies as a check for non-random attrition.

Table 8.1. Variable definitions and descriptive statistics

Variable	Definition	All firms (N=721) mean (std. dev.)	Innovative firms (N=117) mean (std. dev.)	Data source
Margins (*ROR*)	Net profits derived from normal trading activities before tax and interest payments divided by sales	.095 (.0634)	.1049 (.0561)	Datastream item 26, item 104
Innovations (*INN*)	Total number of innovations produced in all innovating units owned by the firm	.0449 (.3041)	.2716 (.7063)	SPRU Innovations tape
Production spillovers (*IPI*)	Total number of innovations produced by all members of the two-digit industry	12.98 (15.23)	16.97 (15.96)	SPRU Innovations tape
Use spillovers (*UI*)	Total number of innovations used by all members of the two-digit industry	6.40 (5.88)	7.37 (5.781)	SPRU Innovations
Unionization (*UN*)	Industry union density by two-digit industries	.6761 (.1168)	.7033 (.094)	Updated from Price and Bain (1983)
Market share (*MS*)	Total firm sales divided by three-digit industry total sales and work done	.0254 (.0682)	.0723 (.1190)	Datastream item 104, and ACOP, Table P1002a
Concentration (*CON*)	Five-firm three-digit industry concentration ratio by sales	.399 (.1776)	.4097 (.1675)	ACOP, Table P1002a
Import intensity (*IMP*)	Imports divided home demands by three-digit industry	.2506 (.1409)	.2625 (.1073)	Business Monitor, Table MQ12

instance, suppose we have a ten-year panel and the model is estimated from year three to year ten. In year three we can (in the absence of serial correlation) use variables dated year one as valid instruments, whilst in year four we can use instruments dated year one and year two, and so on until in year ten any instruments dated year eight or before are valid. Hence, we can generate more efficient estimates by calling on more instruments the further advanced our panel becomes. It is, of course, crucial that we have no serial correlation in the residuals, and we present appropriate tests of this below. We also present statistical tests of the overidentifying restrictions made available by the large instrument set.

3. Innovation and Profitability

The first question that we wish to ask is how large a difference the production of a major innovation makes to the innovation producer's profits. The first four columns of Table 8.2 show estimates of equation (1) under a number of different assumptions. The first three difference out the fixed effects and use instruments for the lagged dependent variable, while the fourth shows OLS estimates without fixed effects. Regression (i) allows only current innovations to affect margins, while (iii) includes six lags in the innovations variable. Regression (ii) is identical to (i) except that market share and its interaction are instrumented (see the notes to the table for more details). Initially we shall focus on regressions (i)–(iii).

All three regressions reveal a (surprising) positive but rather imprecisely estimated effects of unionization and import intensity, and positive, well-determined effects of market share and concentration on profit margins (see also Machin and van Reenen, 1990). In fact, the size of the estimated effect of market share on margins is somewhat sensitive to the assumption of exogeneity of market share. Using the estimates in (i), market shares are positively related to margins for all industries for which $CON < .6195$, while concentration is positively related to margins for all firms for which $MS < .0644$. Only 12 per cent and 9 per cent of the sample of 721 firms have average values of CON and MS above these limits. Using (iii), these limits are $CON < .8353$ and $MS < .0612$, and only 1 per cent and 9 per cent of the sample firms are above them. The coefficient on the lagged dependent variable is very precisely estimated in all three

Table 8.2. Regression on estimates of equation (1)

	(i) Estimate of (1)	(ii) MS instru.	(iii) Incl. lagged INN	(iv) OLS w/o fixed effects	(v) 117 innovators	(vi) 604 non-innovators
Constant	−0.0093 (6.525)	−0.0086 (7.073)	−0.0088 (7.251)	−0.0015 (0.426)	−0.0101 (12.683)	−0.0087 (6.328)
Innovations (INN)	0.0029 (2.817)	0.0036 (5.078)	0.0036 (5.115)	0.0031 (3.002)	0.0033 (9.492)	—
Production spillovers/100 (IPI/100)	0.0003 (0.307)	0.0050 (0.537)	0.0042 (0.453)	0.0074 (1.783)	0.0112 (2.268)	0.0049 (0.473)
Use spillovers/100 (IUI/100)	0.0010 (0.822)	0.0131 (1.253)	0.0126 (1.202)	−0.0039 (0.386)	0.0359 (3.158)	0.0159 (1.472)
Unionization (UN)	0.0046 (0.223)	0.0091 (0.531)	0.0106 (0.613)	0.0037 (0.801)	0.0195 (0.958)	0.0058 (0.353)
Market share (MS)	0.1780 (2.068)	0.3301* (4.786)	0.3823* (5.263)	0.0413 (3.077)	0.0584* (2.582)	0.0862* (0.945)
Concentration (CON)	0.0185 (1.166)	0.0294 (2.193)	0.0280 (2.071)	0.0060 (2.054)	0.0142 (0.994)	0.0202 (1.457)

Table 8.2. (Cont.)

	(i) Estimate of (1)	(ii) MS instru.	(iii) Incl. lagged INN	(iv) OLS w/o fixed effects	(v) 117 innovators	(vi) 604 non-innovators
Market share × Concentration ($MS*CON$)	−0.2873 (1.808)	−0.3601* (3.255)	−0.4577* (3.679)	−0.0681 (2.590)	−0.2315* (5.408)	0.2012* (1.310)
Import intensity (IMP)	0.0188 (1.022)	0.0060 (0.392)	0.0041 (0.266)	−0.0080 (2.201)	−0.0294 (1.880)	0.0037 (0.222)
Margins(−1) ($ROR(-1)$)	0.4978* (14.628)	0.4791* (16.856)	0.4835* (16.932)	0.8691 (60.453)	0.3986* (18.969)	0.4831* (16.073)
Innovations(−1) ($INN(-1)$)	—	—	−0.0005 (0.665)	−0.0026 (2.527)	−0.0010 (2.410)	—
Innovations(−2) ($INN(-2)$)	—	—	0.0008 (0.936)	−0.0004 (0.341)	−0.0004 (0.103)	—
Innovations(−3) ($INN(-3)$)	—	—	0.0012 (1.327)	0.0006 (0.471)	0.0010 (2.878)	—
Innovations(−4) ($INN(-4)$)	—	—	−0.0007 (0.705)	−0.0009 (0.746)	−0.0001 (0.319)	—

Table 8.2. (Cont.)

	(i) Estimate of (1)	(ii) MS instru.	(iii) Incl. lagged INN	(iv) OLS w/o fixed effects	(v) 117 innovators	(vi) 604 non-innovators
Innovations(−5) ($INN(-5)$)	—	—	0.0024 (2.455)	0.0021 (1.907)	0.0022 (6.377)	—
Innovations(−6) ($INN(-6)$)	—	—	0.0013 (1.393)	−0.0001 (0.097)	0.0004 (1.364)	—
No. of firms	721	721	721	721	117	604
Sample size	6 086	6 086	6 086	6 086	1 005	5 081
Serial correlation	−0.795	−0.841	−0.812	−3.245	1.077	−1.757
Sargan (dof)	36.96 (25)	94.58 (77)	94.20 (77)	—	78.72 (77)	94.78 (77)

Notes: The dependent variable is the profit margin, *ROR*. Equations (i)–(iii) and (v)–(vi) are estimated in first-differences using Arenallo and Bond's (1991) instrumental variable estimator. A * superscript denotes an instrumented variable. In (i) the instruments used are $ROR(-2)$ back to $ROR(-4)$ in each time-period. In (ii), (iii), (v), and (vi) *MS* and *MS*CON* are used in the same manner, together with Dividends($t - 2$) and Investment/sales($t - 2$). Absolute values of heteroscedastic-consistent *t*-ratios are given in parentheses below the estimated coefficients. All equations include 8 time-dummies. Sargan is a Chi-square test of the overidentifying restrictions. For the first-differenced models in (i)–(iii) and (v)–(vi) the serial correlation test is an $N(0,1)$ test for second-order serial correlation. In (iv), the levels model, it is an $N(0,1)$ test for first-order serial correlation.

regressions, and suggests that the long-run effects associated with changes in the various exogenous variables are roughly twice the size of their short-run effects.

Both of the spillover variables, *IPI* and *IUI*, have very small positive effects on margins that are imprecisely estimated. That spillovers from the use and production of innovations are small is consistent with earlier work done on productivity growth in the UK using these innovations data (e.g. Geroski (1991*a*), reprinted as Chapter 7 in this volume, but stands in contrast with other work on US firms and industries that has uncovered spillover effects associated with R. & D. expenditures (e.g. Jaffee, 1986; Bernstein and Nadiri, 1988, 1989; Levin, 1988; Levin and Reiss, 1988; and others). There are several possible explanations for this difference in results, including institutional differences in knowledge transmission between the USA and UK and the industry composition of different data-sets. However, our view is that the main difference arises because the US studies used data on research inputs to measure spillovers, while we have used data on research output. Since R. & D. is likely to measure disembodied knowledge (however imperfectly), while our innovation variables measure knowledge embodied in specific commercial products, the different results on spillovers suggest that knowledge in general (as generated by R. & D. programmes) spills over between adjacent producers and users, but not knowledge embodied in the specific products of major innovations. That is, by the time knowledge has been embodied in a major innovation, it is likely to be too use-specific to spill over into many other applications.

The effect of innovations produced on an innovation-producing firm's margins is positive, significant, and quite robust to alterations in the vector of independent variables used. Using (i), the production of one additional innovation has a long-run effect of $0.0036/(1 - 0.4791) = .0058$ on profit margins, raising them by some 6.1 per cent relative to the mean. Using (ii), the long-run effect is estimated to be .0069. Regression (iii) allows for the effect of previous innovations produced on margins, generating a long-run effect of $(0.0036 - 0.0005 + 0.0008 + 0.0012 - 0.0007 + 0.0024 + 0.0013)/(1 - 0.4835) = .0157$ which raises margins by some 16.5 per cent relative to the mean. Since the extra six terms in (iii) cannot be eliminated without significantly reducing the fit (the Wald test is $\chi^2(6) = 14.03$ (*p*-value $= 0.029$)), our inclination is to prefer the estimates in (iii). To help get a handle on what these estimates mean, it is worth noting that in 1980 prices the average total sales of the firms in the sample is £139m., yielding an estimated increase in profits associated with the production of an innovation of just over £2.1m. over the seven years subsequent to its intro- duction.[5] The instantaneous increase in profits associated with innovation is about £500,000. Needless to say, the value of these (major) innovations to their producers far exceeds that of the average patent. Shankerman and Pakes (1986) for example, found the median value of UK patents that survived at least five years to be $1,861.

The effects of innovation on margins proved to be quite ro- bust to a wide range of respecifications on (i). Dropping the other observables yielded long-run estimates of the order of .009, and much the same results emerged when only firm or time-dummies were included in the regression. Dropping the lagged dependent variable raised the estimated coefficient on innovations by 50 per cent, but it also induced serious serial correlation. Rerunning the regression shown in column (iii) using the level of industry R. & D. lagged two and three periods as an instrument for current innovations yielded estimated coefficients (and t-statistics) on current and lagged innovation of: 0.0042 (2.490), 0.0001 (0.054), 0.0013 (0.981), 0.0015 (1.338), −0.0005 (0.453), 0.0025 (2.302), and 0.0015 (1.420), suggesting that assuming innovations to be exogenous may lead to a slight understatement of their effect on profits. Experiments on a smaller sample of 539 firms (the balanced panel) also yielded very similar results as is shown on Table 8.2, allaying fears about sample-selection bias arising from the possibility that non-innovators are less likely to survive. Including a capital– sales ratio in (i) and using a profits–capital-stock ratio as the dependent variable both yielded estimates of profitability dif- ferences similar to those reported above.[6] These estimates of the effects of innovation on margins are also surprisingly in- sensitive to the estimation method used (although the effects of unionization, concentration, import intensity, and the lagged dependent variable are sensitive to estimation technique). For

[5] To check this calculation, we reran (i) using total profits as the dependent variable. The effect of innovation on profits was positive and yielded an estimated increment to profits in the long run associated with one additional innovation of £1.79m. in 1980 prices.

[6] It is well known that accounting profits may diverge from economic profits if the valuation of capital is not handled correctly (although persistently high accounting profits mean that economic profits are also persistently high). We experimented with a transformation of the dependent variable suggested by Fisher (1987: 394), which (under rather restrictive assumptions) overcomes this problem. The results so gener- ated were almost identical to those reported in Table 8.3.

example, regression (iv) shows an OLS respecification of (1) in which the fixed effects are suppressed. This simplification does not much affect the estimates associated with innovations, although it does have extremely noticeable effects on the point estimates associated with market share and concentration. Using instruments proposed by Anderson and Hsiao (1981), rather than the Arellano and Bond method produced similar results to those shown on Table 8.1 in versions of (i)–(iii), but they were estimated with less precision.

The long-run effect of .0157 shown in regression (iii) in Table 8.1 is an average across all firms (or innovations) in the sample. Previous work tracing the effects of innovations sourced from different innovation-producing sectors on users' productivity growth has revealed major interindustry differences in the value of innovations, with those produced in Engineering making a particularly substantial contribution (see Geroski (1991*a*), reprinted as Chapter 7 in this volume. To examine whether the effects of innovation on profitability varies across industries, we ran regression (iii) on subsamples of firms located in various two-digit industry groups. Table 8.3 shows estimates of the long-run effects of innovation on producers' profit margins for each. As one might expect, there is a good deal of heterogeneity in the size of these effects across industry groups. What is somewhat unexpected, however, are the large positive effects in Clothing and Textiles, Paper and Printing, and Bricks and Glass where relatively few innovations are produced, the low effects in Engineering and the negative effects in Chemicals where are both high innovation-producing sectors. Although the fact that larger effects on margins are recorded in sectors where less innovation occurs is (very roughly) consistent with the hypothesis of diminishing returns to innovation, a considerable degree of within-industry variance exists in these estimates. Further, the means shown on Table 8.3 are very sensitive to small reclassifications of firms to the different sectors. We conclude that there is a noticeable degree of heterogeneity in the effects of innovation on profits, but that it is not closely ordered by sector (at least at this broad level of classification).

4. *Innovators and Non-Innovators*

The second question that we wish to ask is whether the differences in profitability between innovators and non-innovators

Table 8.3. Results by industry grouping

Industry	Long-run innovation effect	No. of innovations 1972–83	No. of firms
All firms	$0.0076/(1 - 0.4835) = 0.0147$	377	721
Chemicals	$-0.0024/(1 - 0.4911) = -0.0048$	63	43
Bricks and glass	$0.0059/(1 - 0.5527) = 0.0133$	23	34
Metals and Engineering, of which	$0.0040/(1 - 0.5251) = 0.0085$	229	328
Mechanical Engineering	$0.0215/(1 - 0.5352) = 0.0457$	130	168
Others (Electrical, Instrument, Vehicles, Metals)	$-0.0016/(1 - 0.4753) = -0.0029$	99	160
Food, Drink and Tobacco	$-0.0125/(1 - 0.0496) = -0.0132$	16	72
Clothing and textiles	$0.0431/(1 - 0.2328) = 0.0562$	17	113
Paper and Printing	$0.0126/(1 - 0.3540) = 0.0195$	17	66
Miscellaneous	$0.0046/(1 - 0.1283) = 0.0053$	12	65

Note: Derived from specifications comparable to column (iii) of Table 8.1.

are transitory or permanent; that is, are they associated with the introduction of specific innovations, or are they generic and based on differences in underlying competitive abilities of innovators and non-innovators? The results reported in Section 3 were based on the *product view* of the effects of innovation, and our next step is to explore the *process view*. This rests on the premiss that a firm is best thought of as a bundle of skills and/or distinctive capabilities: competitive advantage arises whenever a firm accumulates a set of skills which more than match those of its rivals. As many of the skills which give rise to competitive advantage are knowledge-based, it follows that learning is likely to be a fundamental element of competitive strategy. Indeed, since knowledge is likely to be most useful only when it is firm-specific, it follows that developing existing skills internal to the firm is likely to be as important as the purchasing of assets in the appropriate factor markets in building up competitive abilities. In this context, the process of innovating may matter because it helps to develop a firm's internal capabilities, enhancing its ability to learn about new technology, to match technological possibilities with the characteristics of demand, and, as a consequence, to sustain its market position in the face of changes in supply and/or demand conditions.[7]

Even a cursory inspection of the data reveals that there are more differences between innovators and non-innovators than the simple fact that the former produced one or more innovations during the period while the latter did not. In particular, an inspection of Table 8.1 reveals that innovators' market shares were nearly six times larger than those of non-innovators (the 1972–83 average total sales of innovators was £460m. in 1980 prices; the average for non-innovators was £76m.). More interesting is the fact that the difference in profits between innovators and non-innovators is not fixed throughout the sample period, as Fig. 8.1 shows. Although a clear difference in profitability is evident at the end of the period, no difference in margins between the two sets of firms is discernible in the first four years of the sample. This observation is particularly interesting because the number of innovations produced by firms in the sample declined throughout the period (see Fig. 8.2). If the

[7] For similar arguments which stress the dual nature of R. & D. as a process which both produces innovative outputs and builds up internal capabilities, see Cohen and Levinthal (1989); Mowery and Rosenberg (1989); Pavitt (1991); Malerba (1992); and others.

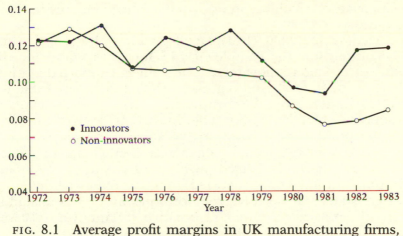

FIG. 8.1   Average profit margins in UK manufacturing firms, 1972–1983

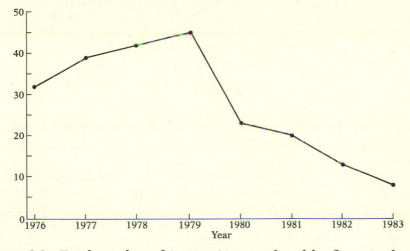

FIG. 8.2   Total number of innovations produced by firms in the sample

product view were the only explanation of how innovation affects profitability, one would expect to see larger profitability differentials between innovators and non-innovators at the beginning of the period, and not at the end. The early 1980s was a period of severe recession in the UK, and the fact that profitability differences seem to be largest then suggests that there may exist generic differences between innovators and non-innovators which become particularly evident only in times of adversity.

To account for what is displayed on Fig. 8.1, we estimated (1) separately for the sample of 117 innovators and for the sample of 604 non-innovators.[8] The split is supported statistically (p-value < .001), and regressions (v) and (vi) in Table 8.1 show estimates for the innovating and non-innovating subsamples which are comparable to (iii). Aside from an effect from the number of innovations produced, the major difference between the two samples lies in the coefficients associated with market share, the lagged profit margin, and the 1980 and 1981 time-dummies (not reported). The estimates of the latter are significant and negative for non-innovators, but insignificantly different from zero and positive for innovators. Even more interestingly, the coefficients on the spillover variables are larger and more significant in the innovators' equation than in the non-innovators' equation.[9] This is consistent with the view that the transmission of knowledge is not costless, that only firms with substantial inhouse research capabilities are likely to be able to benefit from spillovers.

To interpret regressions (v) and (vi), write (1) as $ROR^I = X^I \beta^I + \mu^I$ when applied to the sample of innovators, and as $ROR^N = X^N \beta^N + \mu^N$ when applied to the sample of non-innovators. The predicted profitability differential can be written as: $\hat{D} = \hat{\beta}^I(X^I - X^N) + X^N(\hat{\beta}^I - \hat{\beta}^N)$, where a hat denotes an estimated value. Thus, part of the difference between innovators and non-innovators (which, on average overall, is 0.012) comes from the fact that the latter produce no innovations and have smaller market shares (these may not be independent events), and part comes from the different coefficients on market shares, lagged profits, and the 1980 and 1981 time-dummies (the contribution of the innovation variables is 0.0012, or 10 per cent of the total differential). All of these differences might be classified as 'transitory' to distinguish them from 'permanent' differences that are captured in the fixed effects. Interpreting (v) and (vi) in this

[8] Very similar results were obtained using a balanced panel of 539 firms which contained 98 innovators; see Geroski and Machin (1993*b*).

[9] We also used a dummy variable (innovators = 1, non-innovators = 0) interacted with all the exogenous variables in (iii) in Table 8.1 to help identify which particular exogenous variables differed significantly between innovative and non-innovative firms. Although it proved to be very easy to reject the restriction that all 16 of the dummy-variable interacted terms could be excluded, the variables whose t-statistics were near conventional levels were: the market share–concentration interaction, lagged margins, and all the time-dummies.

way produces the rather strong conclusion that differences in the fixed effects are large and positive (the mean fixed effect for innovators was .048, while that for non-innovators was .030), while transitory effects are small and negative. However, the transitory effects are very noticeably cyclical in impact, and suggest that innovating firms were much more able to maintain margins in the recession of the early 1980s than were their non-innovating counterparts (the transitory predicted differential was .009 higher in 1980–2 than it was on average over the earlier part of the period).[10] Most of this cyclical transitory effect is captured by the 1980 and 1981 time-dummies, but it is also possible to observe a small contribution originating from the market share and innovation variables included in (1).[11]

Thus, profitability differences between innovators and non-innovators seem to reflect inherent generic differences between the two types of firm, but they are difficult to observe accurately because of the effects of a number of transitory cyclical factors. Identifying the source of generic differences is a good deal more difficult than measuring them, but it seems reasonable to believe that the differences in the fixed effects of innovators and non-innovators which we have observed are associated with innovative activity. In particular, regressing the estimated fixed effects on a number of observables suggests that they are higher for innovative firms, and for firms located in heavy innovation-producing sectors (they are lower in heavy innovation-using sectors). Denoting the estimated fixed effects as $\hat{\alpha}_i$, two typical regressions thrown up by this exercise are:

$$\hat{\alpha}_i = \begin{array}{c} 0.030 \\ (24.102) \end{array} + \begin{array}{c} 0.018\,\overline{\text{INOV}}_i \\ (5.624) \end{array}$$

$$\hat{\alpha}_i = \begin{array}{c} 0.034 \\ (3.920) \end{array} + \begin{array}{c} 0.020\,\overline{\text{INOV}}_i \\ (6.000) \end{array} + \begin{array}{c} 0.003(\overline{\text{IPI}/10})_i \\ (2.230) \end{array} - \begin{array}{c} 0.013(\overline{\text{IUI}/10})_i \\ (2.625) \end{array}$$

$$\begin{array}{c} + 0.009\,\overline{\text{UN}}_i \\ (0.658) \end{array} - \begin{array}{c} 0.044\,\overline{\text{MS}}_i \\ (2.363) \end{array} - \begin{array}{c} 0.005\,\overline{\text{CON}}_i \\ (0.578) \end{array} - \begin{array}{c} 0.017\,\overline{\text{IMP}}_i, \\ (1.671) \end{array}$$

[10] It is unlikely that this result arises because innovation-producing firms inhabit sectors which are not very cyclically sensitive, since most of the innovation producers are located in Engineering and Chemicals. However, it is worth stressing that our data contain only one recession, and the results reported in the text may be specific to the early 1980s.

[11] Geroski and Machin (1993*b*) have also observed differences in the growth performance of innovators and non-innovators which are cyclically sensitive; in recessions, non-innovators grow noticeably slower than innovators.

where absolute *t*-ratios are in parentheses, bars denote firm averages, $\overline{INOV}_i$ is a 0–1 dummy indicating whether firm *i* innovated between 1972 and 1983 or not. Including both $\overline{INN}$ and $\overline{INOV}$ yielded

$$\hat{\alpha}_i = \begin{array}{ccc} 0.030 & + \ 0.017\,\overline{INOV}_i & + \ 0.003 \ \overline{INN}_i, \\ (24.076) & (4.618) & (0.479) \end{array}$$

suggesting that it is the fact that innovation occurs and not the total number which occur that is associated with the fixed effects (which is why the OLS estimates of the effect of innovation in column (iv) of Table 8.2 are so similar to those in column (iii)). These results are, of course, consistent with the view that the different profit and innovation record of innovators and non-innovators arises from differences in some deep-seated 'competitive ability' closely linked to the innovation process.

To put these results into perspective, we have made one final set of calculations. The *product view* of innovation looks for effects timed with the production of specific innovation, while the *process view* looks for effects associated with the transformation of a firm's internal capabilities. To assess the relative size of these two effects, we took a 'typical' non-innovator (i.e. one whose exogenous traits were equal to the mean values of the exogenous variables used in (vi) for the subsample of non-innovators, and whose profits were given by the coefficients in (vi)) and transformed it by giving it the attributes of an innovator (i.e. supposing that its profits were determined by regression (v) in Table 8.2). The short-run gain in profits in the year 1975 was £0.4m. (in 1980 prices), and pushing forward to 1983 gives a short-run gain of £4.087m. (evaluated at the innovator's mean values of all exogenous variables). Converting to long-run equivalents gives a gain of £7.135m., some three times the size of the gain to the production of a specific innovation estimated earlier using regression (iii). That is, the effects of innovation on profitability associated with the product of a specific innovation (i.e. those associated with the product view of innovation) considerably understates the total effects of innovation on profits. In the area of innovative activities, it may matter more what a firm does than what it produces.

5. *Conclusions*

In summary, we have uncovered two properties of the data which are worth highlighting. The first is that the number of innovations produced by a firm has a positive effect on its profitability, but one that is, on average, only rather modest in size. It is, of course, possible that this kind of reward is commensurate with the efforts made by the firms themselves. However, to interpret this result properly, it is important to distinguish the returns to the production of innovations from the returns to their use. Relatively few of the innovations in this data-set were first used by the firm that produced them, and (largely anecdotal) evidence suggests that many were developed in close consultation with users. Other research using these data has revealed that these innovations have had a far greater impact on users' productivity growth than on producers' productivity (e.g. Geroski, 1991*a*), and there is no reason not to think that this might also be true with profitability. It follows, then, that the relatively modest profits apparently realized by innovation producers may only be a fraction of the value created by innovative activity.[12] What is more (and what is more surprising), we observe relatively small (and very imprecisely estimated) spillovers associated with the innovations in our data. These apparently small spillovers stand in contrast with much larger spillovers estimated in the USA using data on R. & D. expenditures, and may reflect the fact that disembodied knowledge spills over more easily than knowledge embodied in specific new products.

The second interesting feature of the data is that although innovators seem to enjoy higher profit margins because of the specific innovations which they introduce, substantial permanent differences in the profitability of innovating and non-innovating firms also exist which are not closely timed with the introduction of specific innovations. These permanent profitability differences probably reflect generic differences in 'competitive ability' between innovators and non-innovators, and they seem to be associated in a very general way with the process of innovating. They also enable innovative firms to realize the benefits of spillovers more fully than non-innovative firms. Further, innovating firms enjoy higher margins because they have larger market shares than innovators, and because the margins associated with possessing a market share of a given size are higher for innovating firms. Both of these may

---

[12] On the other hand, the fact that commercial success is one of the criteria used to select innovations into the SPRU data-set means that we are unlikely to uncover negative effects on profitability associated with them. As a consequence, the *total* returns to innovation activity (i.e. to producing successful and unsuccessful innovations) are likely to be lower than those reported in the text.

reflect the indirect effects of the specific innovations introduced by these firms, or they may signal a more fully developed set of internal capabilities. Finally, the profit margins of innovating firms are somewhat less sensitive to cyclical downturns than are those of non-innovators, an observation which adherents of the process view of the effects of innovation are likely to regard as deeply sensible. Whatever it is that creates generic differences between innovators and non-innovators, the consequence is that the former are likely to be quicker, more flexible, more adaptable, and more capable in dealing with market pressures than the latter are. Since these are characteristics which are likely to have most value to their possessor in conditions of severe adversity (e.g. in harsh recessions), it is no surprise to observe that profitability differences between innovators and non-innovators are widest when the going gets rough.

9 Innovation, Profitability, and Growth over the Business Cycle*

1. *Introduction*

Debates about Industrial Policy in the UK are dominated by a concern to make UK firms 'more innovative'. Countless measures of research progressiveness seem to tell the sorry story of a once great industrial power slipping down the international innovation league tables, and each dozen economists who address this problem produce several dozen solutions. Although there is much work yet to be done in measuring social rates of return and assessing the relative efficacy of different policies designed to stimulate innovation, it seems clear that a comprehensive examination of these issues requires one to think carefully about how the performance of innovative firms might differ from that of non-innovative ones. In this chapter we would like to focus directly on this question, and ask 'what effects would one expect to observe on UK corporate performance if UK firms became more innovative?'

As in many other situations, the answer turns out to be sensitive to the way one poses the question in the first place. There are (at least) two alternative views about how innovation might enhance the performance of a firm. The simplest and most

* With Steve Machin; first reprinted in, and reprinted with the permission of, *Empirica*, 20 (1993): 35–50. We are obliged to the ESRC for support. Some of the work discussed here draws upon joint work with John van Reenen, and we are obliged to him for his assistance and helpful comments. Jonathan Haskel also provided very helpful comments on an early draft of the paper. We are also obliged to seminar audiences at the University of Ulster, the University of Manchester, the National Institute of Economic and Social Research, NERA, UMIST, University College London, the Centre for Economic Performance at the LSE, and the Industrial Organization Conference held at Vienna, 24–6 June 1992, for many stimulating observations. However, the usual disclaimer applies.

obvious view is that product or process innovations alter an innovating firm's competitive position against rivals, or strengthen its bargaining power *vis-à-vis* buyers or suppliers. Each innovation is, therefore, likely to have an effect on performance which occurs immediately after its arrival, but this effect is likely to be transitory: profits and growth will be elevated above 'normal' levels for only as long as the innovator can defend itself from rivals. A second and much more subtle view argues that the process of innovation transforms the firm itself, building up its internal capabilities in a variety of ways that create generic differences between innovating and non-innovating firms. This view sees innovation as itself being the consequence of some more fundamental change that transforms a firm's profit and growth performance in both the short and the long term. That is, innovation is an observable signal of a more primal event which has permanent effects on the performance of a firm, effects that do not necessarily manifest themselves only after an innovation occurs. In sum, these two views correspond to the notions that innovation affects corporate performance because the *product* of innovative effort can favourably affect a firm's market position, and because the *process* of innovation can transform a firm's internal capabilities.

Applied econometricians will instantly recognize that these two views of the effects of innovation involve quite different structures of measurement and testing. Adopting the first view leads one to construct models of corporate performance that include, *inter alia*, an innovation variable, and the parameter of interest is the size of the coefficient on that variable. Adopting the second view, however, requires one to entertain the hypothesis that the effects of all of the determinants of corporate performance differ between innovating and non-innovating firms. This, in turn, means that one needs to estimate separate performance equations for each subset of firms, and test whether they differ from each other. In what follows, we shall concentrate on exploring the second view of the effect of innovation on corporate performance (not least because it nests the first), estimating corporate performance equations for innovative and for non-innovative firms. It turns out that there are discernible generic differences between the two types of firms which reveal themselves most clearly during recessions.

The plan of the chapter is as follows. In Section 2, we shall outline the econometric models of corporate performance that we intend to use, and then develop a number of arguments supporting the view that innovation is an observable index of a more fundamental generic difference between different types of firm. In Section 3, we shall describe the data which we have used, and discuss the results of applying our models of corporate growth and profitability to those data. A brief summary and a few concluding observations are contained in Section 4.

2. *Innovation and Corporate Performance*

There are numerous ways to assess corporate performance, and most commentators agree that there is no simple, single measure which captures everything of importance. However, assessing performance using multiple indicators is often made difficult by the conflicting rankings each measure gives of the performance of different firms. For those interested in describing the behaviour of firms, performance measures are of interest because of the incentives that they create for managers, and many commentators express differences in the managerial objective functions of different firms in terms of relative preferences between growth and profitability.[1] It follows that one might legitimately start by focusing on these two measures, and that is the course that we shall pursue here. There are, of course, countless different ways to measure profitability and growth, but many of these different measures of each have similar properties.[2] In what follows, we shall concentrate on profitability measured as a return on sales, and growth measured as the first difference in the log of sales.

Developing models of the effect of innovation (and other exogenous variables)[3] on corporate performance measured either

---

[1] e.g. Odagiri (1992) describes the behaviour of Japanese firms in terms of a preference for growth; more generally, see the survey and discussion in Mueller (1987).

[2] Measuring profitability has been the source of much recent controversy, the problem being that of ensuring that capital inputs are properly valued. This (and other measurement errors) can give rise to large differences between different measures of profitability. However, even when accounting and 'economic' profits do diverge, it is nevertheless the case that persistently high levels of accounting profits imply persistently high levels of economic profits; see Fisher and McGowan (1983), Fisher (1987), and Edwards *et al.* (1987). Measurement problems associated with growth are likely to be no less serious than those associated with profitability, but growth rates are so inherently variable that this additional source of variation is likely to be relatively insignificant; see Hall (1987).

[3] In what follows, we shall presume that innovation is exogenous to current-period growth and profitability. While there is no doubt that firms undertake innovative activities to increase their size and improve their profitability and use past profits to finance current R. & D. efforts, the many lags that occur during the innovation process mean that it is highly unlikely that there exists a strong feedback between current values of profitability and growth on the one hand, and innovation on the other.

as profits or as growth requires one to make two different sets of decisions. The first and most important is the decision about how innovation affects performance, and, as we have seen, there are (at least) two views worth considering in this context: that it is the *product of an innovation* which matters, and that it is the *process of innovation* which matters.[4] The second decision relates to the type of 'experiment' which one needs to conduct in order to observe the effect that one is looking for. If, one believes that it is the *product of innovation* which matters, then an accurate measurement of the effect of innovation on performance requires one to correct for other determinants of performance which might be correlated with innovation, to allow effects to accumulate over time, and so on. If on the other hand, one believes that it is the *process of innovation* which matters, then one needs to decide how to identify the firms who been transformed by this process, and distinguish them from firms who have not. Let us consider each type of decision in turn.

The two views of how innovation might affect performance lead to two quite different types of econometric model. Consider some firm i operating at time t. In an environment characterized by a number of exogenous variables x_{it} and z_{it}, it manages to achieve a profit outcome, π_{it}, and a rate of growth g_{it}. In addition, it may or may not innovate, a state of affairs indicated by positive or zero values of I_{it}. The simplest view of the effect of innovation on performance is that it is transitory and timed to occur with the appearance of specific innovations (referred to as the 'product view' hereafter). This view is embodied in the models

$$\pi_{it} = \beta_0(L)x_{it} + \alpha_0(L)I_{it} + \mu_{it} \tag{1}$$

$$g_{it} = \beta_1(L)z_{it} + \alpha_1(L)I_{it} + \eta_{it}, \tag{2}$$

where the sets of exogenous variables x_{it} and z_{it} may overlap, μ_{it} and η_{it} are white-noise residuals, and the $\beta(L)$'s and $\alpha(L)$'s denote polynomials in the lag operator L. α_0 and α_1 are the effects that one wishes to measure, and are identified whenever

---

[4] It is important not to confuse this distinction between the 'product of' and the 'process of' innovation with the conventional distinction between 'product' and 'process' innovations. It is conceivable that product and process innovations have different effects on profits and growth, but these effects are transitory and associated with the occurrence of a particular innovation of either type. Effects associated with the process of innovation are generic, and can be observed even when innovations are not produced.

the indicator variable I_{it} is positive. Estimates of the coefficients in α_0 and α_1 indicate how transitory the effects of innovation on corporate performance are.

The second view of innovation is that it reflects a generic transformation in how a firm operates (referred to as the 'process view' hereafter). The core notion here is that a firm is best thought of as a bundle of skills and/or distinctive capabilities. Competitive advantage arises whenever a firm accumulates a set of skills which more than match those of its rivals, and competitive strategy describes the choice of both the speed and the direction of this process of accumulation. Since many of the more important skills which give rise to competitive advantages are knowledge-based, it follows that implementing competitive strategies may be as much a matter of learning and developing existing skills internal to the firm as it is of purchasing assets in the appropriate factor markets. The process of innovating affects corporate performance, then, because it helps to develop a firm's internal capabilities, enhancing its ability to learn about new technology, to match technological possibilities with the characteristics of demand, and, as a consequence, to sustain its market position in the face of changes in supply and/or demand conditions.[5]

If it is the process of innovation that matters, then the models of profits and growth embodied in equations (1) and (2) have two major deficiencies. First, the causal presumption that the occurrence of an innovation ($I_{it} > 0$) leads to a (transitory) increase in profits and/or growth makes no sense. When it is the process of innovation (rather than the product of the innovative process) that matters, the effects of innovation which one might expect to observe on profits and growth will occur even when $I_{it} = 0$ at some date t. Indeed, since the primal causal forces affecting a firm's performance are its internal capabilities, one might think of the event $I_{it} > 0$ as no less a consequence of superior competitive ability as high profits or fast growth are. Second, since the process of innovation describes a process by which a firm's capabilities are transformed, it follows that the effects of innovation are as likely to be observed in differences in the β's between innovating and non-innovating firms as they are to be associated with the occurrence

[5] e.g. Cohen and Levinthal (1989) contrast the view of R. & D. as a process which produces innovative outputs with the view of R. & D. as a process which builds up internal capabilities; see also Mowery and Rosenberg (1989), Pavitt (1991), Willman, (1991), and others.

of a specific innovation. That is, innovation is likely to transform the whole process by which profits and growth are generated, and this means that the models of profits and growth described in equations (1) and (2) may differ between innovating and non-innovating firms.

An appropriate way to model the process view of the effect of innovation on corporate performance is as follows. Using the event $I_{it} > 0$ for any t in the sample period to distinguish innovating firms (denoted with a superscript I) from non-innovating firms (denoted with a superscript N) for whom $I_{it} = 0$ throughout the sample period, then

$$\pi_{it}^{I} = \beta_0^{I}(L)x_{it}^{I} + \mu_{it}^{I} \tag{3}$$

$$\pi_{it}^{N} = \beta_0^{N}(L)x_{it}^{N} + \mu_{it}^{N}, \tag{4}$$

and

$$g_{it}^{I} = \beta_1^{I}(L)z_{it}^{I} + \eta_{it}^{I} \tag{5}$$

$$g_{it}^{N} = \beta_1^{N}(L)z_{it}^{N} + \eta_{it}^{N}, \tag{6}$$

where the indicator variable I_{it} may also be an element of the sets x_{it} and z_{it}. The difference in the profits and growth performance of innovating and non-innovating firms is then

$$(\pi^{I} - \pi^{N}) = \beta_0^{I}(x^{I} - x^{N}) + x^{N}(\beta_0^{I} - \beta_0^{N}) \tag{7}$$

and

$$(g^{I} - g^{N}) = \beta_1^{I}(z^{I} - z^{N}) + z^{N}(\beta_1^{I} - \beta_1^{N}), \tag{8}$$

where we have suppressed the subscripts and the distributed lag notation to reduce clutter.

Equations (7) and (8) suggest that differences in the performance of innovating and non-innovating firms may arise from one of two sources. First, the exogenous determinants of profits and growth may differ between the two types of firm (this corresponds to the term in the first set of brackets in (7) and (8)), say because innovating firms have larger market shares or operate in industries where rich technological opportunities affect the ability of firms to make profits and/or grow. Second, innovating firms may perform differently from non-innovating firms because the effects of a given exogenous determinant of profits or growth is different for the two types of firm (this corresponds to the term in the second brackets of (7) and (8)), say because the effects of a given market share or a given technological environment are more readily transformed into a superior profit or growth outcome by innovative firms. Comparing (3)–(6) with (1)–(2), it is clear that the former models generalize the latter by allowing the data to reveal a performance differential in performance which varies across firms and over time. In (1)–(2), innovating firms outperform non-innovating firms simply because $I_{it}^I > 0$ while $I_{it}^N = 0$; (3)–(6) adds to this the possibility of differences in performance associated with a range of further exogenous factors.

The second decision that one must make when modelling the effects of innovation on corporate performance is the nature of the 'experiment' needed to measure the effect one is interested in. The principal consideration of importance is to avoid omitting important exogenous determinants of profitability and growth which are correlated with innovation. Similarly, since we are only interested in measuring the effect of innovation on performance, the omission of important exogenous determinants of profitability or growth is not a major concern if they are not correlated with innovative activity. The literature on the determinants of innovation often focuses on the role played by firm size and market structure, and many scholars believe that innovative activity is pro-cyclical. Hence, we include variables reflecting cyclical shifts in economic activity, and variables measuring the salient features of market structure. In addition, innovations produced or used by one firm may have an effect on the performance of other firms through spillovers, and these spillover effects need to be allowed for.[6]

These considerations have led us to specify the vector of variables x_{it} in (1) as: current and lagged values of the number of innovations produced by firm i, INN_{it}, spillover variables measuring the number of innovations used and the number of innovations produced by firm i's rivals (in the same three-digit industry), IPI_{it} and IUI_{it}, the degree of concentration, import penetration, and unionization in firm i's industry, CON_{it}, IMP_{it}, and UN_{it}, firm i's market share, MS_{it}, an interaction variable between market share and concentration, a lagged dependent variable to capture disequilibrium dynamics, and a full set of firm-specific and time-dummies to control for other omitted

---

[6] See Cohen and Levin (1989), for a survey of empirical studies of the determinants of innovation. Much of this work suggests that the role of firm size and market structure in affecting innovation is fairly modest, and is probably dominated by the effects of variations in 'technological opportunities'. For a survey of work on spillovers, see Geroski (1992).

factors.[7] The vector of variables z_{it} in (2) includes: current and lagged values of the basic variable of interest, INN_{it}, the two spillover variables, IPI_{it} and IUI_{it}, firm-size lagged, $SIZE_{it}$, several lags of the dependent variable, and current and lagged values of industry and aggregate growth rates, Ig_{it} and Ag_{it}.[8] By and large, these specifications encompass most of the work reported in the literature that has worked with equations like (1) and (2).

3. *Innovating and Non-Innovating Firms*

Most of the basic data that we will be working with are described on Table 9.1, which also provides a brief characterization of innovating and non-innovating firms. The basic variable of interest is the innovativeness of each firm, and the data that we have used are a count of major innovations produced and used in the UK over the period 1945–83 constructed by the Science Policy Research Unit at the University of Sussex (for further details, see Chapter 2). The selection criteria used by SPRU to assemble this database were that the innovation had to be both a technical breakthrough and a commercial success.[9] The data-tape records somewhat in excess of 4,000 major innovations over the period 1945–83, but less than 10 per cent of these were produced by our sample of 539 firms over the period 1972–83. Using this information on innovativeness, we

[7] For a justification of the market share–concentration interaction variable, see Kwoka and Ravenscraft (1986), Machin and van Reenen (1992), and others; Geroski and Jacquemin (1988), and Mueller (1986) and (1990) make the case for allowing for dynamics explicitly in a model like (1). Fixed effects are included to pick up relatively permanent factors which affect the profitability of firms, and might be best interpreted as (indirect) measures of the height of mobility barriers. The time-dummies are designed to capture macroeconomic effects which all firms feel. For a fuller discussion, see Geroski *et al.* (1993), repr. as Ch. 8 in this volume.

[8] The inclusion of a size variable has been standard in growth equations for some time, and reflects an interest in testing the Law of Proportionate Effects. The inclusion of lagged dependent variables, industry growth, and aggregate growth rates is designed to capture unobserved firm, industry, and macroeconomic shocks, and the persistence of the effects of these shocks on firm growth can be untangled from the estimated coefficients on these observables. Firm-specific effects are not included because there is very little persistence in corporate growth rates over time; see Geroski and Machin (1993*a*) and references cited therein for a fuller discussion.

[9] That these innovations are selected into the sample because (*inter alia*) they are commercial successes means that we are unlikely to see negative effects on corporate performance associated with them. If these innovations are set against those that were introduced but failed, then the returns to total innovative activities are likely to be lower than those estimated below.

Table 9.1. The characteristics of innovating and non-innovating firms, 1976–1983

Variable	Description	The full sample (539 firms)	Innovators (98 firms)	Non-innovators (441 firms)	Source
g	First difference in the log of sales	.1083	.1132	.1072	Datastream, Item 104
ROR	Net profits derived from normal trading activities before tax and interest payments divided by sales	.0953	.1043	.0932	Datastream, Item 26, Item 104
INN	Total number of innovations produced in all innovating units owned by the firm	.0513	.2819	0.0000	SPRU Innovations tape
IPI	Total number of innovations produced by by all members of the two-digit industry	12.580	15.948	11.831	SPRU Innovations tape
IUI	Total number of innovations used by all members of the two-digit industry	6.279	7.207	6.073	SPRU Innovations tape
UN	Industry union density across 15 two-digit industries	.6815	.7084	.6755	Updated from Price and Bain (1983)
MS	Total sales divided by industry total sales work done	.0282	.0797	0.168	Datastream, Item 104, ACOP, Table P1002a
CON	Five-firm concentration ratio by sales	.3952	.4033	.3933	ACOP, Table P1002a
IMP	Import intensity, defined relative to home demand	.2548	.2671	.2520	Business Monitor, Table MQ12
SIZE	Defined as the log of firm sales (t − 1)	3.2644	4.7762	2.9285	Datastream, Item 104
Ig	First difference in the log of industry sales	0.0972	0.0990	0.0970	ACOP, Table P1002a
Ag	Aggregate real GDP growth	0.0165	0.0165	0.0165	Economics Trends

partitioned the data into one subset of ninety-eight firms who produced a major innovation during the period (about 18 per cent of the sample), and a second subset of 441 firms who did not.[10]

The means displayed on Table 9.1 suggest that innovating firms operate in more innovative sectors (that is, sectors in which large numbers of innovations were produced and/or used), and may, therefore, be exposed to more spillovers than non-innovative firms. Innovative firms in our sample are slightly more likely to be unionized than non-innovators, at least partly because they operate in slightly more concentrated industries than non-innovators. It is not, however, unambiguously clear that innovative firms operate in less competitive markets than non-innovators, since import penetration is relatively high in the markets which innovators inhabit. All of these differences are fairly small however, and they all pale into relative insignificance when compared to what seems to be the truly substantive difference between innovators and non-innovators in this sample: namely that the former have market shares which are, on average, just under five times larger than those enjoyed by the latter.[11]

The top two rows of Table 9.1 show that there are, on average, modest performance differences between innovative and non-innovative firms. The former enjoy profits about 11.9 per cent larger than the latter, and their rate of growth is about 5.6 per cent higher. One must, however, be slightly careful about interpreting these differences for three reasons. First, there is a considerable variation in growth rates across the sample that should make one rather wary of reading too much into differences in means. The difference in mean profit margins between the two groups is about 18 per cent of the standard deviation across the whole sample, while the mean difference in growth rates is about 3 per cent of the full sample standard deviation

[10] Relatively few of the innovations recorded in this data-set were first used by the firm that produced them. That is, the data only identify innovation-producing firms, and there are good grounds for thinking that users capture many of the benefits yielded by these innovations (see Geroski (1991a), repr. as Ch. 7 in this volume. It follows that however accurately our estimates measure the effects of these innovations on innovation-producing firms, they are likely to understate the total effects of these innovations on the profits and growth of all of the firms who are associated with them.

[11] The relationship between firm size and innovativeness across all firms and innovations in the *SPRU* data-tape is more complex than this, since very small firms contribute disproportionately to total innovative activity (see Pavitt *et al.*, 1987). What Table 9.1 shows is a pro-Schumpeterian positive correlation between size and innovation within the (sub) population of large, quoted firms.

in growth rates (both profit and growth rates are approximately normally distributed).[12]

Second, comparing means in this way attributes all of the difference between the two groups to the fact that the one group of firms produced at least one innovation during the sample period, while the other did not. In fact, work on this and similar samples using (1) and (2) applied to a group of innovating and non-innovating firms suggests that the simple comparison shown in Table 9.1 understates the effects of innovation on both profits and growth. In particular, Geroski *et al.* (1993), reprinted as Chapter 8 in this volume, used a slightly larger sample of firms and found that each additional innovation produced raised margins by 1.57 percentage points, some 16.5 per cent relative to the mean. The instantaneous increase in total profits associated with each additional innovation was £400,000, rising to some £1,500,000 in the longer run. Using the current sample of firms, Geroski and Machin (1993*a*) found that the production of a single innovation raised growth rates by 1.4 percentage points in the long run, an increase of just under 13 per cent relative to the sample mean.

The third reason why the data displayed in Table 9.1 must be read with care is that Table 9.1 fails to capture what is arguably the most interesting feature of the data. This is displayed on Figs. 8.2, 9.1, and 9.2. Fig. 8.2 shows the total number of innovations produced by firms in the full sample over the period. The important point to note is that the total number of innovations produced by firms in our sample falls off markedly towards the end of the period, dropping from a high of forty-five in 1979 to a low of seven in 1983. Using (1) or (2), one would immediately infer from this that differences in profits and growth between innovating and non-innovating firms are likely to have decreased during the period: one would expect to see much larger differences in profits and growth between the two subsets of firms in the middle 1970s than in the early

[12] Growth rates are far more variable than profits and the range over which they vary is several times larger. What is more—and what is more interesting—most of the variation in growth rates is within-firm variation while most of the variation in profitability is between firms (with percentage of variation that is within-firm is 86 per cent for growth and 7 per cent for profits). This lack of persistence in growth over time is particularly evident when one looks at the serial correlation in the data. The correlation between growth rates in 1982 and 1983 is −0.056, and falls to −0.026 between growth rates in 1974 and 1983; for profitability, the same correlations are 0.914 and 0.459. We have also used robust regression methods to downgrade the importance of outliers in our growth equations, but the resulting estimates were very similar to those reported in the text.

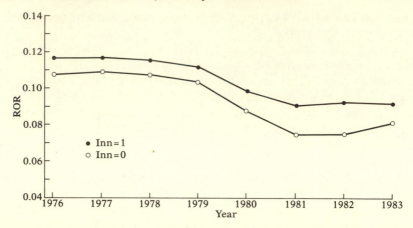

FIG. 9.1   Total number of innovations produced by firms in the sample

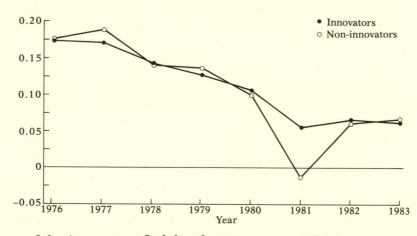

FIG. 9.2   Average profitability for innovators and non-innovators

1980s. Figs 9.1 and 9.2 show that the average profit and growth rates for the two types of firms throughout the period do not conform to this pattern. Profit differences are rather smaller at the beginning of the period (the difference is .008 in 1976) than they are at the end (the differences were .016, .018, and .011 in 1981, 1982, and 1983), while the difference in growth rates is negligible in virtually every year except 1981. In fact, what emerges most clearly from Figs 9.1 and 9.2 is that the perform-ance differences between innovators and non-innovators are most noticeable during recessions.

It seems evident, then, that modelling the effect of innovations on corporate performance using equations (1) and (2) misses what seems to be the most intriguing feature of the data: namely that performance differences between innovating and non-innovating firms are not constant over time and, in particular, are not closely correlated with variations in the total volume of innovative activity. There are, of course, numerous potential causes of this non-constancy in performance differentials, and it seems natural to turn to equations (3)–(6) to help identify them.

Table 9.2 reports estimates of equations (3) and (4). Comparing equations (3) and (4) to estimates of a similarly specified equation (1) leads one to reject the null hypothesis that the differences between the estimates of (3) and (4) are not significant (asymptotic p-value for the appropriate Wald test < 0.001); that is, (1) is not an acceptable simplification of the system (3)–(4). The results shown in Table 9.2 suggest that each innovation produced by an innovating firm has a short-run impact on profitability of 0.23 of a percentage point (raising profitability by just over 2 per cent relative to the mean profitability of innovators), and a long-run effect of 0.006 (raising profitability by 5.8 per cent relative to the mean profitability of innovators, and 6.4 per cent relative to non-innovators). Innovation spillovers seem to be rather modest in size, and their size is imprecisely determined in both samples. Like many other studies, we find that market share has a positive and significant impact on profitability, as does industrial concentration for non-innovators (it is statistically insignificant in the innovators subsample). Industry unionization takes opposite signs but is not very well determined in both cases, whilst import penetration and the market share–concentration interaction exert a negative effect in both samples. Probably the two most important differences between innovators and non-innovators are the coefficients on the lagged dependent variable and on the time-dummies. Lagged profitability has a precisely determined effect in both samples, but it is evident that the dynamics of profitability differ significantly between the two types of firm. In particular, the long-run impact of any exogenous variables, x_{it}, on the profitability of innovating firms is about 1.25 times larger than its short-run effect; for non-innovating firms, long-run effects are twice as large as short-run effects.[13] The second noticeable difference

[13] i.e. the profitability of innovating firms is less persistent over time (all else constant) than that of non-innovators, although variations in innovators' profits are not noticeably less predictable than those of non-innovators.

Table 9.2. Models of profitability estimated using (3) and (4)

	(i) Innovating firms	(ii) Non-innovating firms
Constant	0.0015(0.810)	0.0084 (4.764)
INN	0.0023(3.804)	—
IPI/100	0.0078(0.736)	−0.0047 (0.370)
IUI/100	0.0031(1.812)	0.0061 (0.412)
UN	0.072 (1.853)	−0.0385 (1.741)
MS	0.2205(2.916)	0.4743 (3.871)
CON	0.009 (0.222)	0.1518 (3.735)
MS×CON	−0.4822(4.012)	−0.7781 (3.677)
IMP	−0.0480(3.686)	−0.0207 (1.458)
ROR (−1)	0.1950(4.710)	0.5601(15.311)
INN (−1)	−0.0008(1.319)	—
INN (−2)	0.0001(0.121)	—
INN (−3)	0.0007(0.946)	—
INN (−4)	−0.0004(0.507)	—
INN (−5)	0.0021(2.897)	—
INN (−6)	0.0009(1.224)	—
D1977	−0.0026(0.980)	−0.0039 (1.515)
D1978	−0.0037(1.631)	−0.0112 (5.655)
D1979	−0.0069(3.530)	−0.0093 (5.068)
D1980	−0.0144(5.587)	−0.0140 (6.767)
D1981	−0.0047(1.198)	−0.0130 (5.339)
D1982	0.0065(1.584)	−0.0024 (0.832)
D1983	0.0021(0.644)	−0.0045 (1.767)
Average fixed effect	0.037	0.008
No. of firms	98	441
Sample size	784	3528

Notes: The estimation period is 1976–83; absolute *t*-statistics in parenthesis; these regressions include firm-specific fixed effects, and the variables D_n are dummy variables isolating particular years n.

concerns the common macroeconomic effects captured by the time-dummies, especially in the early 1980s. The sum of the time-dummy coefficients between 1980 and 1982 is −0.0126 for innovators and −0.0294 for non-innovators; converted to long-run analogues these become −0.0156 and −0.0668 respectively. That is, the early 1980s recession saw a more marked fall in the margins of non-innovators (relative to trend profitability) than in the margins of innovating firms, suggesting that innovators

Table 9.3. Models of sales growth estimated using (5) and (6)

	(iii) Innovating firms	(iv) Non-innovating firms
Constant	0.039(1.364)	0.028(2.198)
SIZE	−0.002(0.710)	−0.004(1.552)
g (t−1)	0.097(2.043)	0.080(3.229)
g (t−2)	0.032(0.457)	−0.017(0.800)
g (t−3)	0.097(2.565)	0.054(1.793)
INN (t)	0.009(1.256)	—
INN (t−1)	−0.007(0.976)	—
INN (t−2)	0.001(0.137)	—
INN (t−3)	0.008(1.077)	—
Ig (t)	0.171(2.190)	0.120(3.055)
Ig (t−1)	0.252(3.710)	0.187(5.011)
Ig (t−2)	0.070(1.074)	0.150(3.521)
Ig (t−3)	−0.125(1.426)	0.013(0.336)
IPI/100 (t)	0.061(0.614)	0.117(2.085)
IPI/100 (t−1)	0.039(0.283)	0.013(0.191)
IPI/100 (t−2)	−0.122(0.682)	−0.079(0.981)
IPI/100 (t−3)	0.055(0.578)	−0.087(1.326)
IUI/100 (t)	0.349(1.949)	0.104(1.282)
IUI/100 (t−1)	−0.175(0.944)	−0.024(0.324)
IUI/100 (t−2)	0.220(1.437)	0.063(0.903)
IUI/100 (t−3)	−0.278(1.863)	0.015(0.221)
Ag (t)	0.177(0.384)	0.230(1.183)
Ag (t−1)	0.092(0.180)	1.587(7.277)
Ag (t−2)	−0.204(0.470)	−1.201(6.332)
Ag (t−3)	0.031(0.104)	0.352(2.551)
R^2	0.114	0.128
No. of firms	98	441
Sample size	784	3328

Notes: The estimation period is 1976–83; absolute *t*-statistics in parentheses; these regressions do not include firm fixed effects.

were more able to insulate themselves during this severe downturn than non-innovators were.

Turning to corporate growth, Table 9.3 displays estimates of equations (5) and (6). Comparing (5) and (6) to estimates of a similarly specified equation (2) once again leads one to reject the null hypothesis that the differences between the two types of firms shown in Table 9.3 are not statistically significant (asymptotic p-value for Wald-test <0.001). Table 9.3 shows that each innovation produced by an innovating firm has a short-run effect on growth of just under 1 percentage point (raising growth by 8 per cent relative to the mean growth of innovators), and a long-run effect of 1.4 percentage points (raising growth by 12.4 per cent relative to the mean growth rate of innovators, and by 13 per cent relative to that of non-innovators). Innovation spillovers are positive, but small and very imprecisely estimated. The lagged sales growth variables have positive and fairly precisely determined effects, and it is evident that the dynamics of growth do not differ too much between innovating and non-innovating firms: the long-run effects on growth of a change in any exogenous variable z_{it} is 1.3 times larger for innovating firms but only 1.13 times larger for non-innovating firms. However, the most noticeable difference between the two types of firms is in their sensitivity to macroeconomic shocks. An industry-specific shock that increases industry growth rates by 1 per cent raises the growth rate of innovative and non-innovative firms by about 0.5 percentage points. However, a macroeconomic shock which increases aggregate growth raises the growth rate of innovative firms by a mere .124 percentage points; the growth of non-innovative firms increases by 1.09 percentage points.

Using (7) and (8) to decompose the differences between innovators and non-innovators shown in Tables 9.2 and 9.3 adds relatively little to what we have already observed. Most of the profit difference emerges from differences in the fixed effects of the two types of firms (0.037 for innovators and 0.008 for non-innovators), although relatively permanent positive differences are associated with market share and unionization. However, a clearly cyclical component to this difference is evident in the time-dummies, and the recession year of 1981 stands out as a year in which profit differences between innovators and non-innovators are relatively large. In fact, the sum of the coefficients on the 1981, 1982, and 1983 year dummies contributes 0.4 of a percentage point to the mean differential (which is about 1.0 percentage point). Differences in growth performance, by contrast, are more difficult to discern (the mean growth differential is 0.006), and they are not permanent. Most of the difference becomes manifest in 1981, and the most sizeable effect is captured by differences in the coefficients on the aggregate growth variables. These indicate that a 1 per cent fall in real GDP increases the growth differential by 1.6 percentage points (or 200 per cent).[14]

4. *Some Conclusions*

In order to make progress in assessing the magnitude of the effects of innovation on corporate performance, one needs to know how such effects occur. We have contrasted two views of the effect of innovation—the *'product view'* and the *'process view'*—and have provided some evidence to suggest that both effects are evident in the data. Although it is clear that individual innovations themselves have a positive (if fairly modest and perhaps rather short-lived) effect on profitability and growth, it is equally clear that the process of innovation seems to transform firms in some way that gives rise to what look like generic differences between innovators and non-innovators. As a consequence, the process by which profitability and growth are generated differs noticeably between the two types of firms. Perhaps the clearest of these differences is that innovating firms seem to be much less sensitive to cyclical shocks than non-innovating firms are.

There is something deeply sensible and unsurprising about this result (at least when it is looked at with the benefit of hindsight). Whatever it is that creates a generic difference between innovating and non-innovating firms, the result is likely to be that innovators are more flexible and adaptable. They have the internal capabilities to respond quickly to new technological developments, and to bring technological possibilities into harmony with changing consumer needs. One suspects that in many cases, they have organizational structures designed to cope with the challenge of change. If one thinks of the economic environment as a selection mechanism and asks: 'when are these kinds of characteristics likely to increase a firm's survival value?' the answer is, 'almost certainly during times of adversity'. In particular, recessions are a major exogenous change in a firm's market environment, and coping with a recession often requires a fundamental reorientation of

---

[14] Since most of the innovations in the SPRU data come from engineering or chemicals firms, it is unlikely that the (relative) cyclical insensitivity of innovating firms which we have observed arises because innovators are in cyclically less turbulent markets than non-innovators.

a firm's activities. If the innovation process really does transform a firm's internal capabilities, then one would only ever expect to see the effects of this transformation during periods of adversity. Most firms, innovative or not, can prosper in a buoyant market, but only a few of the more innovative ones can continue to do so when the going gets tough.

10 Some Reflections

1. *Introduction*

The substance of this book is the seven individual studies contained in Chapters 3–9. They represent a slightly unsystematic and definitely incomplete exploration of the relationship between innovation, market structure, and corporate performance. Although these studies have some value taken individually, the premiss underlying this book is that they also have some value when considered as a group. My goal in this chapter is to provide some substance for this assertion. In particular, I should like to close the volume with some personal and slightly speculative reflections stimulated by the various results reported earlier. I shall group these under five headings: the relationship between competition and innovation; the relationship between corporate performance and innovation; spillovers and the interindustry flow of knowledge; and policy implications.

2. *Competition and Innovation*

Perhaps the most unusual result uncovered in this work is the reasonably strong and robust negative relationship between market concentration and innovation reported in Chapter 4. Most of the other work which has been done on the relationship between concentration and innovation has uncovered a positive (but not always significant) correlation between the two, and, for this reason alone, the result must be treated circumspectly (for recent surveys of other work, see Baldwin and Scott, 1986, Cohen and Levin, 1989, Cohen, 1992, Scherer, 1992, and others). Statistically speaking, it arises from the technique used to correct for variations in 'technological opportunity'

I am obliged to David Stout for helpful comments on an earlier draft of this chapter.

across industries (i.e. from the use of fixed effects), and it persists even when the positive indirect effects of monopoly power on expected post-innovation returns are controlled for (similar effects on the correlation between R. & D. intensity and firm size have been reported by Cohen *et al.*, 1987). If one accepts this result, then the positive correlation between concentration and innovative activity that is usually reported in the literature must be interpreted as suggesting that concentrated industries are more innovative largely because industries with rich 'technological opportunity' tend to be highly concentrated. That is, highly concentrated industries are more innovative despite— and not because of—the fact that they are highly concentrated.

There are at least three reasons why I am inclined to accept the results reported in Chapter 4. First, the results do not rely only on a correlation between levels of market concentration and innovation, but, rather, on a consistent pattern of correlations between six measures of competitiveness and innovation. The negative correlation between innovation and concentration is persuasive because it is consistent with the positive correlations between innovation and both small-firm activity and entry on the one hand, and the negative correlations between innovation and import intensity, changes in concentration, and exit on the other. Second, and in the same spirit, there is a good deal of complementary evidence which suggests that both small firms and new entrants are important producers of new innovations. Some of that evidence was discussed in Chapters 2 and 5 respectively, and it is consistent with results reported elsewhere in the literature (see Acs and Audretsch, 1990, and others). Intuitively, one expects to see relatively higher levels of small-firm and entrant activity in less concentrated sectors, and this means that the positive correlation between innovation and small-firm activity or entry on the one hand, and the negative one between innovative activity and concentration on the other may be mirror images of the same phenomenon. Third and finally, there is no doubt that it is 'technological opportunity' and not market competitiveness which is the major determinant of the output of the innovation process. Although it is not entirely clear that the technique which I used adequately controls for this important set of omitted variables, it is certainly the case that fixed effects do a better job in this respect than most of the proxies for technological opportunity commonly used in the literature.

The results reported in Chapter 4 are also relatively easy to accept because it is not difficult to believe that they are true. Almost by definition, 'major' innovations threaten existing market structures, and, as a consequence, small firms or fringe players have an incentive to use them to improve their market position, while large incumbent firms who enjoy rents on their existing activities have an incentive to resist their advance. Although large, monopolistic firms may have superior resources to generate new innovations and may be in a better position to exploit them than other firms, innovative activity is often rent-displacing and this dulls the incentives of such firms to innovate. Superior opportunities do not count for much if agents have little incentive to exploit them.

The correlation between market structure and innovation is often thought of as a test of 'the' Schumpeterian hypothesis, although it is doubtful that Schumpeter himself would see things in exactly this way. Another strand of thinking which might also be attributed to Schumpeter is the view that innovations are deconcentrating, that 'gales of creative destruction' lead to the displacement of market leaders and create turbulence in market shares. Although there are arguments which suggest that innovation may increase market concentration in the long run (for an interesting discussion of the relationship between the evolution of product/process technology and market structure which points to a concentrating effect of innovation, see Utterbeck and Suarez, 1993), the results reported in Chapter 3 are consistent with the view that (at least) the short-run effect of innovations introduced by small firms or new entrants on industry concentration is negative. These results are not strongly out of line with a variety of hints which have appeared in the literature on this subject. Taken together, these results paint a picture of positive feedback between decreases in market concentration and increases in innovativeness: innovations gradually and very slowly deconcentrate markets and, in so doing, they gradually and very slowly increase the level of innovative activity which they exhibit.

It is worth noting that it is almost certainly the case that small-firm and entrant activity drives the negative association between changes in concentration and innovative activity which appears in the data. Work on the effects of innovation on the market shares of leading firms (i.e. firms ranked in the top five of each industry) reveals clearly that the production of new innovations has a strong and robust positive effect on the market share of the innovation-producing firm (see Davies and Geroski,

1993), and unusually high levels of innovative activity are associated with relatively infrequent rank changes amongst market leaders in UK industry (see Geroski and Toker, 1993). It follows from this that industries which produce many new innovations tend to deconcentrate largely (it seems) because market leaders often fail to keep up with the innovative pace set by smaller or entrant firms. Those firms—leaders and fringe players alike—who do innovate however, are usually able to improve their market share as a consequence.

It would be a serious mistake to push these results too hard. Everyone can think of examples of very innovative monopolists, or of markets whose consolidation was powered by a string of major innovations. The pattern of correlations which we have identified in the data reveal only broad tendencies, and it would be imprudent to claim that the broad tendencies which we have isolated are overpoweringly strong. What the data do suggest is that innovative monopolists are impressive performers not only because they innovate, but also because they do so in circumstances which often retard the innovativeness of their monopolistic brethren. Further, it is not inconceivable that the impressive innovative performance of some monopolists would actually be more impressive if they were exposed to somewhat more competition. The important point, however, is that there is no evidence to support the usual presumption that reducing levels of market concentration will always increase allocative efficiency at the expense of dynamic efficiency. Breaking up strong monopoly positions or injecting a little life into cosy oligopolies is almost always likely to improve their performance in both the short and the long run.

3. *Corporate Performance and Innovation*

It is not hard to believe that innovation improves the performance of firms, and stimulates productivity growth in the industries they inhabit. The real question is, of course, how large these effects are and how quickly they materialize. The evidence that we have generated on these questions is contained in Chapters 6 and 7, and it shows that the production and use of major innovations explains a fairly large percentage of total factor-productivity growth. Equally unsurprising but perhaps more interesting, the evidence indicates that users seem to enjoy most of these benefits. This probably arises from some of the particular features of the innovation process in Engineering, which is the major innovation-producing sector in our data. There is some reason to think that appropriability conditions may be weak in this sector (see Section 4 below), and the small firms who produce most of the innovations in Engineering may be particularly disadvantaged when bargaining with users. It may also be the case that the links between innovation producers in Engineering and their users in other industries are particularly rich, and the distribution of the gains from producing new innovations may actually reflect the relative importance of inputs by the two parties into the innovation process.

The evidence which we have uncovered on the effects of innovation on corporate performance is contained in Chapters 8 and 9. The interesting results here are not so much the size of the effect that innovation has, as how it manifests itself. In this context, we distinguished effects arising from the *product of the innovation process* from those associated with the *process of innovating*. New product or process innovations affect the market position of firms, altering the conditions of cost and demand which they face. These changes translate into noticeable but fairly modest effects on the profitability and (less clearly) the growth of innovation producers (wages also seem to be higher on average in innovation-producing firms; see van Reenen, 1993). Our estimates are not out of line with those reported in studies of the effects of patenting activity on corporate performance (see Griliches, 1990, for a recent survey), and they probably understate the effects of innovation on corporate performance. More speculatively, the process of producing an innovation transforms the internal resources of the firms themselves, altering their ability to react to various types of cost and demand shocks. Our data showed fairly clearly that innovating firms (i.e. those who produced at least one innovation during the sample period) significantly outperformed non-innovators during the recession which occurred in the UK during the early 1980s. Indeed, our calculations reveal that the total gains to innovating sometime in the early 1970s are completely dominated by the performance differences between innovators and non-innovators which opened up during the recession.

There are at least three observations of interest which spring from these results. First, the work in Chapters 8 and 9 traces the effects of innovation only on the performance of innovation-producing firms. Since the results reported in Chapter 7 on industry-productivity growth suggests that users capture many of the benefits generated by these innovations, it seems reasonable to believe that the effects on corporate performance which we have uncovered significantly understate the total surplus created by these innovations. Particularly interesting in this respect is the finding, reported in Chapter 9, that the short- and long-run effects on corporate growth associated with each new innovation produced are very similar. One hazards the guess that, for many of the innovations in the data (particularly those sourced from Engineering), the role of producers is largely confined to producing some specific piece of output (i.e. some type of capital good) which is purchased in very limited quantities by users but then applied to a wide range of downstream operations. If this is the case, then our results almost certainly miss much of the interesting action associated with these major innovations.

Second, the time-period over which we traced the effects of these innovations is rather short, and it is arguably the case that the 'long-run' estimates generated by our models are, in fact, really only the tip of the iceberg. Tracing the effects of these innovations on firm performance over a much longer time-horizon might uncover subtle but much more pervasive consequences springing from investments in innovative activity. The problem arises because many of the costs of producing an innovation are known and incurred upfront, while revenues are generated in the future, often in unexpected ways. Using a short times-series captures many of the costs, but may miss some of the revenues.

The observation that econometricians may understate the net effects of producing an innovation applies equally strongly to decisions-makers within a firm. When an innovation produced by one particular firm is augmented by subsequent innovations produced by rivals, it often opens up a new market (or market niches) which develops slowly and in unexpected ways. More generally, users of new products and processes often are slow to perceive, and then to learn how to use an innovation, and this also means that the net benefits of a new innovation may accrue for very long periods of time, and in ways impossible to imagine *ex ante*. If revenues are difficult to anticipate, then risk-averse firms will systematically understate their size (particularly if accountants get involved in the calculations). Since these revenues arise in the future, the effect is analogous to double discounting (although it is really a failure of imagination), and may lead firms to seriously underinvest in innovative activities.

Third, the distinction drawn between the *product of the inno-vation process* and the *process of innovating* suggests a second reason why managers (and analysts) may often understate the benefits of innovation. It is one thing to accurately assess the effects of a particular innovation on a firm's market position, but it is an altogether different thing to trace the subtle, much more intangible effects that the production of an innovation has on the capabilities of an innovation-producing firm. That the process of producing an innovation makes a firm more perceptive, flexible, and adaptable (amongst other things, ena-bling it to benefit more extensively from spillovers) is probably uncontroversial, but it is less than clear when such benefits will manifest themselves and how big they really are. It is not hard to believe that many firms will simply ignore such considera-tions in their net benefit calculations, and this may be a pru-dent course to follow (intangibles are notoriously easy to exaggerate). If one accepts the proposition that such enhanced abilities are particularly useful in adverse circumstances, then one expects to see such benefits manifesting themselves mainly in periods of crisis (like recessions). Our calculations suggest that these benefits are relatively large, but this is hardly the last word on the subject.

As something of a digression, it is worth noting that the work reported in Chapters 8 and 9 raises a number of interesting issues about measuring corporate performance. What is par-ticularly striking in the comparison between corporate profit-ability and corporate growth is the fact that the two vary in quite different ways across firms and over time. Most notice-able is the fact that growth rates are much more variable than profitability across firms and over time. More interesting, profit-ability differences between firms are very persistent over time, while the growth rates of most firms varies more over time then they do across firms at any given time. That is, the total variation in profitability across firms and over time is domin-ated by 'between-firm' variations, while the total variation in corporate growth is dominated by 'within-firm' variation. By contrast, innovative activity has some between-firm variation which arises from the fact that many firms never innovate, and some within-firm variation arising from the fact that most in-novating firms innovate only sporadically. Taking the three variables as complementary (but perhaps not exhaustive) indi-cators of 'corporate performance' creates something of a puz-zle, since no two of them paints the same picture of how particular firms perform over time or relative to their rivals.

None of the work reported in this volume really provides much of a basis for calculating the social rate of return to innovative activities. At best, the results which suggest that users appropriate a large share of the benefits of innovation point to a potentially serious divergence between private and social rates of return. What matters, of course, is whether the share of the returns claimed by users is proportionate to their contribution to the innovation process, and there is no hard information on this in our data. However, the work reported above does suggest that private rates of return may often be seriously underestimated both by managers making decisions about how much to invest in innovative activities, and by applied econometricians assessing their decisions. While a gap between social and private rates of return is likely to lead firms to invest 'too little' in innovation activities, it is also the case that any tendency for firms to systematically understate the private rate of return to innovation will have the same effect. The extent to which one or both of these two problems has led firms to do 'too little' innovation is not, as yet, clear.

4. *Spillovers*

One of the interesting features of the work reported in Chapters 7, 8, and 9 is the apparent lack of spillovers generated by the innovations in the data-set. In particular, the inclusion of innovation counts produced or used in closely related industries, or by rivals in the same industry, failed to produce strong or precisely estimated effects on industry productivity growth, corporate profitability, or corporate growth. The sole exception to this conclusion is that spillover variables did register positive and broadly significant effects on the profitability of innovating firms (i.e. those who innovated at least once during the sample period). This result seems to be peculiar to this particular database, since analogous studies using R. & D. expenditures in the USA have uncovered fairly strong evidence that spillovers affect corporate performance (see Bernstein and Nadiri, 1989, Bernstein, 1988, Levin and Reiss, 1988, and others).

The most obvious difficulty with accepting this conclusion is that the technique used to detect spillovers in these studies is rather crude. Although Census industry classifications are built up around identifying groups of firms that use similar production processes, that does not mean that they collect together the firms who are most likely to benefit from one another's spillovers. New innovations often cut across existing industry boundaries, and new ideas are often applied in a range of different guises in a number of different sectors. What one would ideally like to do is find some independent method of identifying the 'technological base' underpinning the operations of a firm, and then use this information to collect firms together into different 'technological clusters' and establish the proximity of each cluster to all of the others (see Griliches (1979) and Dosi (1988) for stimulating discussions of how to detect spillovers and, more generally, the nature of knowledge flows in the economy). For example, Jaffee (1986) located more than 500 US firms into one of twenty-one different 'technological clusters' using information on the type of patent or patent class produced by each. The resulting allocation of firms to technological clusters looked rather different from that obtained using more conventional industry classifications. Using these technological clusters, Jaffee was able to construct measures of the total 'R. & D. pool' available for spillovers, and showed that they had a noticeable effect on several dimensions of corporate performance. The bottom line, then, is that our rather crude technique for detecting spillovers undoubtedly creates serious measurement error problems which may cause us to understate the degree of spillovers associated with the SPRU innovations.

Nevertheless, it is not hard to believe that the spillovers generated from the innovations in our data really are fairly modest, and that it is innovating firms who are most likely to benefit from them. What is more, it is not entirely clear that spillovers, however large or small they are, seriously undermine incentives to innovate. Consider each of these propositions in turn.

As noted in Chapter 2, one way to think of the difference between R. & D. expenditures and innovation counts as measures of innovative activity is that the former measure research inputs, while the latter measure output. A second, slightly different way of characterizing the relationship between the two is to observe that R. & D. expenditures are generally designed to produce knowledge (often of a fairly general nature), while innovations result from the successful embodiment of knowledge in specific products or processes. As the innovation process progresses from R. & D. activity to its final culmination in a specific new product or process, the knowledge that is generated gradually becomes more firmly embodied in a specific product or process and, therefore, becomes more use-specific.

The consequence is likely to be a lessening in the volume of spillovers produced by innovation producers and then used by other firms. It is, therefore, not unreasonable to believe that proxies for innovation activity like R. & D. appear to be associated with more extensive spillovers than proxies like innovation counts.

This does not, of course, mean that the innovations in our data generated no spillovers. Rather, what we observe as 'no spillovers' may be a consequence of the fact that the specialized nature of the knowledge embodied in these innovations effectively restricts the number of agents who are potentially able to benefit from those spillovers which do occur. Indeed, the number of agents who are actually capable of benefiting from such spillovers is likely to be smaller still (Levin *et al.* (1987), for example, reported that most firms believe that only a few of their rivals are capable of duplicating new processes and products). To perceive and then to understand bits of knowledge thrown up from the actions of others often requires a firm to invest heavily in its own research capabilities. In fact, investments in R. & D. may as reasonably be motivated by a desire to build up internal corporate capabilities or to steal secrets from rivals as they are by the prospect of producing new product innovations (in the phrase used by Cohen and Levinthal (1990) they build up a firm's 'absorptive capacity'). It may, therefore, be the case that those firms most able to benefit from spillovers are those least in need of them.

Thus, it seems worth distinguishing between the total potential amount of spillovers which any given bit of knowledge might generate, and those actually received by agents. Further, both the potential and the actual amount of spillovers which occur are likely to vary during different phases of the innovation process, as knowledge becomes more use-specific and more firmly embodied in particular new products or processes. Finally, it is not hard to believe that proven innovators are more likely to benefit from spillovers than less innovative firms. The implication of all of this is that the importance of spillovers may be easy to exaggerate, and, as a consequence, that their effect on incentives to innovate may be much less profound than is usually believed. Two further arguments add weight to these conjectures, and both arise from the inspection of the data reported in Chapter 2.

The first argument is straightforward. What is particularly surprising and interesting about the innovations contained in our data is how few of them were first used by the firm that produced them. Further, the work reported in Chapter 7 suggests that users appear to benefit more from these innovations than producers do. The point is that, unlike spillovers, the information flows which accompany the transfer of these innovations from producers to users do not necessarily undermine incentives to innovate. In fact, much of the knowledge which passes between firms is managed, and yields returns which both firms who are party to the transaction share in one form or the other. Licensing agreements and technology trading are obvious examples of managed information flows, but the one which often seems to be of most importance in many sectors (and in Engineering in particular) is that which occurs when users and producers co-operate to produce an innovation. By contrast, spillovers are unintentional, undirected flows of knowledge which pass between agents, and it is their diffuseness (as much as anything) which makes it hard for econometricians to detect their existence and hard for innovation producers to appropriate some of the benefits realized by those who use them.

Indeed, when producers and users of an innovation co-operate, it is differences in the ability of different agents in the value chain to appropriate the rewards of innovation (e.g. to control spillovers) which are likely to determine whether it is user-, supplier-, or manufacturer-led (see von Hippel, 1982). Users seem to be important in Engineering sectors like Scientific Instruments, Silicon-based Semiconductors, and Electronic sub-assemblies on Printed Circuits. In these sectors, users often first perceive the need for a specific innovation and build the prototype. Manufacturers, on the other hand, typically only perform product engineering work to improve reliability and manufacturability (von Hippel, 1976). By contrast, manufacturers often play a leading role in the innovation process in Engineering Plastics, and suppliers dominate the innovation process in Wire-Termination Equipment, New Engineering Polymers, and new additives for Commodity Plastics. More generally, users are likely to innovate when the structure of the producing industry is very competitive, and when scale economies in the production or use of an innovation are modest. They also have inherent advantages in appropriating the returns from process innovations, not least because (unlike manufacturers) users need not sell a process innovation to benefit from it.

The implication of all of this is that although spillovers can be an important source of knowledge flows between firms, they may not be the most important type of knowledge flow. Further, other types of knowledge flow—such as that between innovation users and producers—may not have the deleterious effect on incentives to innovate that spillovers are widely thought to have. There are good (but not overpoweringly persuasive) reasons for thinking that this might be the case with the innovations contained in our data.

The second argument is less straightforward. As we noted in Chapter 2, the major innovation producers in the UK are, by and large, Engineering firms (followed at a distance by Chemicals firms), and they are, by and large, relatively small. Their small size—and the relatively unconcentrated state of many Engineering sectors—suggests that these innovation-producing firms may experience real difficulties in appropriating the benefits generated by the innovation-producing activities. Further, work by Levin *at al.* (1987) suggests that the effectiveness of process and product patents is much lower in sectors like Semiconductors, Scientific Instruments, and other Engineering sectors than they are in Drugs, Petroleum Refining, and Chemicals. Taken together, these observations create a puzzle: why is it that the Engineering is a more substantive producer of innovations than Chemicals (or Rubber and Plastics) where conditions of appropriability appear to be rather stronger?

Needless to say, there are at least two ways to answer this question. On the one hand, the fact that Engineering produces many innovations despite relatively weak conditions of appropriability may be taken to suggest that the recorded innovation output originating from this sector is a substantial under-realization of its innovative potential. Engineering could—and should—have produced more innovations, in this view. However, the same fact may also be read to suggest that the existence of spillovers and generally weak conditions of appropriability do not seriously undermine the incentive of firms to innovate (see also Levin, 1988). This will almost certainly be the case whenever the pool of agents able to benefit from potentially large spillovers is rather small, or when spillovers between a small group of firms complement (and do not displace) existing inhouse research activity. It may also be the case that the research productivity of large innovation-producing sectors is so great as to overwhelm the disincentives created by spillovers. Finally, it may be that spillovers—however large they are—do not, in fact, constitute a major source of information for rival firms. As noted above, this may be because it is the flows of information between information users and producers that really matter, or it may be that many firms regard independent R. & D. as a major source of information about rivals' technology (as suggested in Levin *et al.*, 1987).

5. *Industrial Policy towards High-Technology Sectors*

It is difficult to draw strong conclusions for public or business policy from much of the foregoing. One obvious problem is that the ratio of questions raised to questions answered in this book is uncomfortably high. More substantively, however well suited the use of innovation counts is for those interested in looking at the effect of innovative activity on market outcomes, it tells us nothing useful about the relationship between innovative inputs and innovative output. This is, of course, a subject of particular importance for the design of policy, and our work casts almost no useful light on it at all. Nevertheless, there are two general observations about policy which seem worth making, and I propose to close the volume by briefly touching upon each in turn.

The first observation concerns the fairly strong tradition of policy-thinking that the moulding or manipulating of market structures might provide an important spur to innovative activity. Anti-trust authorities are often anxious to avoid deconcentrating markets where large firms are likely to be particularly progressive, and a number of national industrial policies have been built up around the use of 'national champions' in particular sectors. The allure of this type of policy initiative is, however, surprisingly easy to resist (see also Scherer, 1992). Not only is it hard to believe that large size and monopoly power are necessary to sustain or even stimulate the innovation process, it is also hard to believe that market structure has anything other than a second-order effect on innovative output. A far more important determinant of innovative output, it seems, is the condition of 'technological opportunity' in particular sectors. Further, the basic competencies and skills of innovating firms are likely to matter more in determining the outcome of any particular innovation project than the number of rivals or the condition of competition which firms expect to face downstream.

What lies beneath the strategy of manipulating the structure of product markets to stimulate innovation is the concern that rivalry and the spillover of information between rivals will affect incentives to innovate. Whenever externalities between firms create market failures which lead to 'too little' (or, less plausibly, 'too much') investment in R. & D., one natural solution is to amalgamate firms together in a way which enables them to internalize such externalities. National champions, co-operative R. & D. ventures, patents, and other devices can all be thought of as *horizontal strategies* (because their scope is limited to the market in which the innovation is produced). The major problem with such strategies is that by restricting competition, they are liable to undermine incentives to invest in R. & D. By contrast, *vertical strategies*, which focus on affecting the market conditions faced by upstream and downstream agents who make an important contribution to the innovation process, seem to be relatively more attractive. The virtues of such strategies include the possibility that they focus policy attention on the important flows of information (e.g. that between innovation users and producers), and they ensure that innovative activity will not be held up by any failures in the markets responsible for providing specialized inputs (see Geroski, 1992).

The second observation also concerns the use of structural measures to stimulate innovativeness, but it more focused on policies related to firm size. The notion that size is a determinant of competitive strength is a myth which is widely—and somewhat inexplicably—believed, and it reveals itself in a number of practices. The interest in national champions is one practical manifestation of this type of thinking; the concentration of procurement contracts into the hands of a few leading firms in high-technology sectors is another. Aside from the fact that the evidence does not unambiguously justify such beliefs, this view embodies a rather oddly implausible presumption about knowledge flows. It is widely understood that successful innovation is a coupling process that matches users' needs with technological possibilities, and it is also widely understood that this coupling process generates important flows of information. What is not obvious is why these flows of knowledge are best managed within firms; that is, why the boundaries of a firm should be drawn to include all of the major information providers or receivers critical to a particular innovation project.

It seems much more appealing to think of 'networks' as being the right unit of observation in the innovation process, and not 'firms'. As our data seem to show, many firms do not use the innovations which they produce, and common sense suggests that there is often no reason why they should. If innovation really is a coupling process, then the appropriate unit of analysis ought to be the 'network' of major contributors and not specific firms, and policy should focus on the infrastructure of firms as much as it does on firms themselves. Further, policies designed to facilitate the formation—and smooth functioning—of groups of firms around specific projects seem to be more sensible than those which try to construct—or reconstruct—firms to match the needs of particular projects. Amongst other things, this suggests that co-operative R. & D. ventures might be a better policy tool to use than sponsoring mergers to the same end (see Geroski, 1993).

One way or the other, the bottom line seems to be that the structure of markets and the size (and internal structure of firms) are not the major determinants of innovative activity, and should not, therefore, be a major focus of technology policy.

References

Abernathy, W., and Utterback, J. (1975), 'A Dynamic Model of Process and Product Innovation', *Omega*, 3: 639–56.

Acs, Z., and Audretsch D. (1987), 'Innovation, Market Structure and Firm Size', *Review of Economics and Statistics*, 69: 567–75.

—— —— (1988), 'Innovation in Large and Small Firms', *American Economic Review*, 78: 678–90.

—— —— (1990), *Innovation and Small Firms* (MIT Press, Cambridge, Mass.).

Aigner, D., Hsiao, C., Kaptegn, A., and Wansbeek, T. (1984), 'The Latent Variable Models in Econometrics', in G. Griliches and M. Intrilligator (eds.), *Handbook of Econometrics* (North Holland, Amsterdam).

Amemiya, T., and McCurdy, T. (1986), 'Instrumental Variable Estimation of an Error-Components Model', *Econometrica*, 54: 869–81.

Anderson, T., and Hsaio, C. (1982), 'Formulation and Estimation of Dynamic Models Using Panel Data', *Journal of Econometrics*, 18: 47–82.

Arellano, M., and Bond, S. (1991), 'Some Tests of Specification for Panel Data: Monte Carlo Evidence and an Application to Employment Equations', *Review of Economic Studies*, 58: 277–98.

Arrow, K. (1962), 'Economic Welfare and the Allocation of Resources for Inventions', in R. Nelson (ed.) *The Rate and Direction of Inventive Activity* (Princeton University Press, Princeton, NJ).

Bain, J. (1956), *Barriers to New Competition* (Harvard University Press, Cambridge, Mass.).

Baldwin, J., and Scott, J. (1987), *Market Structure and Technological Change* (Harwood Academic Publishers, London).

Baumol, W., Panzar, J., and Willig, R. (1982), *Contestable Markets and the Theory of Market Structure* (Harcourt, Brace Jovanovich, New York).

Beesley, M., and Hamilton, R. (1984), 'Small firms Seedbed Role and the Concept of Turbulence', *Journal of Industrial Economics*, 33: 217–32.

Berndt, E., and Fuss, M. (1986), 'Productivity Measurement with Adjustments for Variations in Capacity Utilization and Other Forms of Temporary Equilibrium', *Journal of Economics*, 33: 7–29.

Bernstein, J. (1988), 'Costs of Intra and Inter Industry R. & D. Spillovers: Canadian Evidence', *Canadian Journal of Economics*, 21: 324–47.

—— and Nadiri, M. (1988), 'Inter-industry R. & D. Spillovers, Rates of Return and Production in High-Tech Industries', *American Economic Review*, Papers and Proceedings, 78: 429–34.

—— —— (1989), 'Research and Development and Intra-industry Spillovers: An Empirical Applications of Duality Theory', *Review of Economic Studies*, 56: 249–69.

Blair, J. (1974), *Economic Concentration* (Harcourt, Brace and Jovanovich, New York).

Blundell, R., and Meghir, C. (1987), 'Bivariate Alternatives to the Tobit Model', *Journal of Econometrics*, 34: 179–200.

Bresnahan, T. (1986), 'Measuring the Spillovers from Technical Advance: Mainframe Computers in Financial Services', *American Economic Review*, 76: 742–55.

Bruno, M. (1984), 'Raw Materials, Profits and the Productivity Slowdown', *Quarterly Journal of Economics*, 99: 1–29.

—— and Sachs, J. (1982), 'Input Price Shocks and the Slowdown in Economic Growth: The Case of UK Manufacturing', *Review of Economic Studies*, 49: 679–706.

Cameron, A., and Trivedi, P. (1986), 'Econometric Models based on Count Data: Comparisons and Applications of Some Estimators and Tests', *Journal of Applied Econometrics*, 1: 29–54.

Carlsson, B. (1984), 'The Development and Use of Machine Tools in Historical Perspective', *Journal of Economic Behaviour and Organisation*, 5: 91–114.

Caves, R., and Davies, S. (1987), *Britain's Productivity Gap* (Cambridge University Press, Cambridge).

—— and Porter, M. (1980), 'The Dynamics of Changing Seller Concentration', *Journal of Industrial Economics*, 29: 1–15.

Cockburn, I., and Griliches, Z. (1988), 'Industry Effects and Appropriability Measures in the Stock Markets Valuation of R. & D. and Patents', *American Economic Review*, Papers and Proceedings, 78: 419–23.

Cohen, W. (1992), 'Empirical Studies of Innovative Activity and Performance', forthcoming in P. Stoneman (ed.), *Handbook of the Economics of Innovation and Technical Change* (Basil Blackwell, Oxford).

—— and Klepper, S. (1992), 'The Anatomy of Industry R. & D. Distributions', *American Economic Review*, 82: 773–99.

—— and Levin, R. (1989), 'Empirical Studies of Innovation and Market Structure', in R. Schmalensee and R. Willig (eds.), *Handbook of Industrial Economics* (North Holland, Amsterdam).

—— —— and Mowery, D. (1987), 'Firm Size and R. & D. Intensity: A Re-Examination', *Journal of Industrial Economics*, 35: 543–66.

—— and Levinthal, D. (1989), 'Innovation and Learning: The Two Faces of R. & D.', *Economic Journal*, 99: 569–96.

—— —— (1990), 'Absorptive Capacity: A New Perspective on Learning and Innovation', *Administrative Science Quarterly*, 35: 128–52.

Comanor, W. (1964), 'Market Structure, Product Differentiation and Industrial Research', *Quarterly Journal of Economics*, 81: 639–57.

Curry, B., and George, K. (1983), 'Industrial Concentration: A Survey', *Journal of Industrial Economics*, 31: 203–56.

Dasgupta, P. (1986), 'The Theory of Technological Competition', in F. Mathewson and J. Stiglitz (eds.), *New Developments in the Analysis of Market Structures* (Macmillan, London).

—— and Stiglitz, J., (1980*a*) 'Uncertainty, Industrial Structure and the Speed of R. & D.', *Bell Journal of Economics*, 11: 1–28.

—— —— (1980*b*) 'Industrial Structure and the Nature of Innovative Activity', *Economic Journal*, 90: 266–93.

Davidson, J., and Hendry, D. (1981), 'Interpreting Econometric Evidence: the Behaviour of Consumer's Expenditure in the UK', *European Economic Review*, 16: 177–98.

—— —— Sarba, F., and Yeo, S. (1978), 'Econometric Modelling of the Aggregate Time Series Relationship Between Consumers Expenditure and Income in the UK', *Economic Journal*, 88: 661–92.

Davies, S. (1980), 'Minimum Efficient Scale and Seller Concentration: An Empirical Problem', *Journal of Industrial Economics*, 28: 287–301.

—— and Geroski, P. (1993), 'Changes in Concentration and the Dynamics of Market Shares', mimeo (London Business School).

Diebold, F., and Nerlove, M. (1989), 'The Dynamics of Exchange Rate Volatility: A Multivariant Latent Factor Arch Model', *Journal of Applied Econometrics*, 4: 1–21.

Dosi, G. (1988), 'Sources, Procedures and Micro-economic Effects of Innovation', *Journal of Economic Literature*, 26: 1120–71.

Edwards, K., and Gordon, T. (1984), 'Characterization of Innovations Introduced on the US Market in 1982', Report for the US Small Business Administration by the Futures Group.

Edwards, J., Kay, J., and Mayer, C. (1987), *The Economic Analysis of Accounting Profitability* (Oxford University Press, Oxford).

Farber, S. (1981), 'Buyer Market Structure and R. & D. Effort: A Simultaneous Equations Model', *Review of Economics and Statistics*, 63: 336–45.

Fellner, W. (1951), 'The Influence of Market Structure on Technological Progress', *Quarterly Journal of Economics*, 65: 556–77.

Fisher, F. (1987), 'On the Misuse of the Profits-Sales Ratio to Infer Monopoly Power', *Rand Journal of Economics*, 18: 384–97.

—— and McGowan, J. (1983), 'On the Misuse of Accounting Rates of Return to Infer Monopoly Profits', *American Economic Review*, 73: 82–97.

Futia, C. (1980), 'Schumpeterian Competition', *Quarterly Journal of Economics*, 94: 675–95.

Geroski, P. (1989), 'Entry, Innovation and Productivity Growth',

Review of Economics and Statistics, 71: 572–78; repr. as Ch. 6 in this volume.

—— (1990), 'Innovation, Technological Opportunity and Market Structure', *Oxford Economic Papers*, 42: 586–602; repr. as Ch. 4 in this volume.

—— (1991*a*), 'Innovation and the Sectoral Sources of UK Productivity Growth', *Economic Journal*, 101: 1438–51; repr. as Ch. 7 in this volume.

—— (1991*b*), 'Entry and the Rate of Innovation', *Economics of Innovation and New Technology*, 1: 203–14; repr. as Ch. 5 in this volume.

—— (1992), 'Vertical Relations Between Firms and Industrial Policy', *Economic Journal*, 102: 138–47.

—— (1993), 'Antitrust Policy Towards Cooperative R. & D. Ventures', *Oxford Review of Economic Policy*, 9: 58–71.

—— (1994), 'Markets for Technology', forthcoming in P. Stoneman, (ed.), *Handbook of the Economics of Innovation and Technical Change* (Basil Blackwell, Oxford).

—— and Jacquemin, A. (1988), 'The Persistence of Profits: An International Comparison', *Economic Journal*, 98: 375–90.

—— and Machin, S. (1993*a*), 'The Dynamics of Corporate Growth', mimeo (London Business School).

—— —— (1993*b*), 'Innovation Profitability and Growth over the Business Cycle', *Empirica*, 20: 35–50; repr. as Ch. 9 in this volume.

—— —— and Van Reenen, J. (1993), 'The Profitability of Innovating Firms', *Rand Journal of Economics* 24: 198–211; repr. as Ch. 8 in this volume.

—— and Masson, R. (1987), 'Dynamic Market Models in Industrial Organization', *International Journal of Industrial Organization*, 5: 1–14.

—— —— and Shaanan, J. (1987), 'The Dynamics of Market Structure', *International Journal of Industrial Organization*, 5: 93–100.

—— and Pomroy, R. (1990), 'Innovation and the Evolution of Market Structure', *Journal of Industrial Economics* 38: 299–314; repr. as Ch. 3 in this volume.

—— and Stewart, G. (1991), 'Competitive Rivalry and the Response of Markets to Innovative Opportunities', in S. Arndt and G. McKenzie (eds.), *The Flexibility of the UK Economy* (Macmillan, London).

—— and Toker, S. (1988), 'Picking Profitable Markets', mimeo (London Business School).

—— —— (1993), 'The Turnover of Market Leaders in UK Manufacturing: 1979–1986', mimeo (London Business School).

—— and Walters, C. (1993), 'Innovative Activity Over the Business Cycle', mimeo (London Business School).

Geweke, J. (1977), 'The Dynamic Factor Analysis of Economic Times-Series Models', in D. Aigner, and A. Goldberger (eds.), *Latent Variables in Socio-Economic Models*, North-Holland (Amsterdam, 1977).

Gilbert, R., and Newberry, D. (1982), 'Pre-emptive Patenting and the Persistence of Monopoly', *American Economic Review*, 72: 514–26.

Gort, M., and Kanakayama, A. (1982), 'A Model of Diffusion in the Production of an Innovation', *American Economic Review*, 72: 1111–20.

—— and Klepper, S. (1982), 'Time Paths in the Diffusion of Innovations', *Economic Journal*, 92: 630–53.

Granger, C. (1969), 'Investigating Causal Relations by Econometric Models and Cross-Spectral Methods', *Econometrica*, 37: 424–38.

Greer, D., and Rhoades, S. (1976), 'Concentration and Productivity Changes in the Long and Short Run', *Southern Economic Journal*, 43: 1031–44.

Griliches, Z. (1979), 'Issues in Assessing the Contribution of R. & D. to Productivity Growth', *Journal of Economics*, 10: 92–116.

—— (ed.) (1984), *R. & D. Patents and Productivity* (University of Chicago Press, Chicago).

—— (1990), 'Patent Statistics as Economic Indicators', *Journal of Economic Literature*, 28: 1661–707.

—— and Lichtenberg, F. (1984*a*), 'Inter-industry Technology Flows and Productivity Growth', *Review of Economics and Statistics*, 66: 324–9.

—— —— (1984*b*), 'R. & D. and Productivity Growth at the Industry Level: Is there Still a Relationship?', in Z. Griliches (ed.), *R. & D., Patents and Productivity* (University of Chicago Press, Chicago).

—— and Mairesse, J. (1984), 'Productivity and R. & D. at the Firm Level', in Z. Griliches, (ed.), *R. & D., Patents and Productivity* (University of Chicago Press, Chicago).

—— and Pakes, A. (1984), 'Estimating Distributed Lags in Short Panels with an Application to the Specification of Depreciation Patterns and Capital Stock Contracts', *Review of Economic Studies*, 51: 243–62.

Grossman, G., and Helpman, E. (1991), *Innovation and Growth in the Global Economy* (MIT Press, Cambridge, Mass., 1991).

Hall, B. (1987), 'The Relationship between Firm Size and Firm Growth in the US Manufacturing Sector', *Journal of Industrial Economics*, 35: 583–606.

Hall, R. (1988), 'The Relation Between Price and Marginal Cost in US Industry', *Journal of Political Economy*, 96: 921–47.

Hannah, L., and Kay, J. (1977), *Concentration in British Industry* (Cambridge University Press, Cambridge).

Hart, P., and Clarke, R. (1980), *Concentration in British Industry* (Cambridge University Press, Cambridge).

Hausman, J., Hall, B., and Griliches, Z. (1984), 'Econometric Models for Count Data with an Application to the Patents–R. & D. Relationship', *Econometrica*, 52: 909–38.

—— and Taylor, W. (1981), 'Panel Data and Unobservable Individual Effects', *Econometrica*, 49: 1377–98.

Holz-Eakin, D., Newey, W., and Rosen, H. (1988), 'Estimating Vector Autoregressions with Panel Data', *Econometrica*, 56: 1371–95.

Hughes, K. (1984), 'Determinants of R. & D. Expenditure in UK Manufacturing Industry', mimeo (University of East Anglia).

Jaffee, A. (1986), 'Technological Opportunity and Spillovers of R. & D.: Evidence from Firm's Patents, Profits and Market Value', *American Economic Review*, 76: 984–1001.

Jorgenson, D., and Griliches, Z. (1967), 'The Explanation of Productivity Growth', *Review of Economic Studies*, 34: 249–83.

Judge, G., Griffiths, W., Hill, R., and Lee, T. (1980), *The Theory and Practice of Econometrics* (Wiley & Sons, New York).

Kamien, M., and Schwartz, N. (1982), *Market Structure and Innovation* (Cambridge University Press, Cambridge).

Kilpatrick, A., and Naisbitt, B. (1988), 'A Disaggregated Analysis of the Slowdown in Productivity Growth in the UK Manufacturing Industry in the 1970s', *Oxford Bulletin of Economics and Statistics*, 50: 230–41.

Klapinsky, R. (1983), 'Firm Size and Technical Change in a Dynamic Context', *Journal of Industrial Economics*, 32: 39–60.

Kleinknecht, A. (1987), 'Measuring R. & D. in Small Firms: How Much Are We Missing?', *Journal of Industrial Economics*, 36: 253–6.

Kwoka, J., and Ravenscraft, D. (1986), 'Cooperation v. Rivalry: Price-cost Margins by Line of Business', *Economica*, 53: 351–63.

Lach, S., and Shankerman, M. (1989), 'The Interaction Between Capital Investment and R. & D. in Science-Based Firms', *Journal of Political Economy*, 97: 880–904.

Lee, T., and Wilde, L. (1980), 'Market Structure and Innovation: A Reformulation', *Quarterly Journal of Economics*, 94: 429–36.

Levin, R. (1978), 'Technical Change, Barriers to Entry and Market Structure', *Economica*, 45: 347–61.

—— (1988), 'Appropriability, R. & D. Spending and Technological Performance', *American Economic Review*, Papers and Proceedings, 78: 424–8.

—— Cohen, W., and Mowery, D. (1985), 'R. & D. Appropriability, Opportunity, and Market Structure: New Evidence on the Schumpeterian Hypothesis', *American Economic Review*, 75: 20–4.

—— Klevorick, A., Nelson, R., and Winter, S. (1987), 'Appropriating the Returns from Industrial Research and Development', *Brookings Papers on Economic Activity*, 3: 783–831.

—— and Reiss, P. (1984), 'Tests of a Schumpeterian Model of R. & D. and Market Structure', in Z. Griliches, (ed.), *R. & D., Patents and Productivity* (University of Chicago Press, Chicago).

—— —— (1988), 'Cost Reducing and Demand Creating R. & D. with Spillovers', *Rand Journal of Economics*, 19: 538–56.

Levy, D. (1985), 'Specifying the Dynamics of Industry Concentration', *Journal of Industrial Economics*, 34: 55–68.

—— (1987), 'The Speed of the Invisible Hand', *International Journal of Industrial Organization*, 5: 79–92.

Loury, G. (1979), 'Market Structure and Innovation', *Quarterly Journal of Economics*, 93: 395–410.

Lunn, J., and Martin, S. (1986), 'Market Structure, Firm Structure and R. & D.', *Quarterly Review of Economics and Business*, 26: 31–44.

Machin, S., and Van Reenen, J. (1993), 'Profit Margins and the Business Cycle: Evidence from UK manufacturing Firms', *Journal of Industrial Economics*, 41: 29–50.

Malerba, F. (1992), 'Learning by Firms and Incremental Technical Change', *Economic Journal*, 102: 845–59.

Mansfield, E. (1984), 'R. & D. and Innovation: Some Empirical Findings', in Z. Griliches (ed.), *R. & D., Patents and Productivity* (University of Chicago Press, Chicago).

—— Rapopart, J., Romeo, A., Wagner J., and Beardsley, G. (1979), 'Social and Private Rates of Return from Industrial Innovations', *Quarterly Journal of Economics*, 91: 221–40.

Mendis, L., and Muellbauer, J. (1984), 'British Manufacturing Productivity 1955–1983: Measurement Problems, Oil Shocks and Thatcher Effects', mimeo (CEPR, London).

Mowery, D., and Rosenberg, N. (1989), *Technology and the Pursuit of Economic Growth* (Cambridge University Press, Cambridge).

Mueller, D. (1986), *Profits in the Long Run* (Cambridge University Press, Cambridge).

—— (1987), *The Corporation: Growth, Diversification and Merger* (Harwood Academic Publishers, London).

—— (ed.) (1990), *The Dynamics of Company Profits* (Cambridge University Press, Cambridge).

—— and Rogers, R. (1980), 'The Role of Advertising in Changing Concentration of Manufacturing Industries', *Review of Economics and Statistics*, 62: 89–96.

Mukhopadhyay, A. (1985), 'Technological Progress and Change in Market Concentration in the US, 1963–1977', *Southern Economic Journal*, 52: 141–9.

Nickell, S. (1981), 'Biases in Dynamic Models with Fixed Effects', *Econometrica*, 49: 1417–26.

—— (1985), 'Error Correction, Partial Adjustment and all that: an Expository Note', *Oxford Bulletin of Economics and Statistics*, 47: 119–29.

Odagiri, H. (1992), *Growth Through Competition, Competition Through Growth* (Oxford University Press, Oxford).

Ornstein, S., Weston, J., Intrilligator, M., and Shrieves, R. (1973), 'Determinants of Market Structure', *Southern Economic Journal*, 39: 612–25.

Pakes, A. (1985), 'On Patents, R. & D., and the Stock Market Rate of Return', *Journal of Political Economy*, 93: 390–409.

—— (1986), 'Patents as Options: Some Estimates of the Value of Holding European Patent Stocks', *Econometrica*, 54: 755–84.

Patel, P., and Pavitt, K. 'Patterns of Technological Activity: Their Measurement and Interpretation', forthcoming in P. Stoneman, (ed.), *Handbook of the Economics of Innovation and Technical Change* (Basil Blackwell, Oxford).

Pavitt, K. (1991), 'Key Characteristics of the Large Innovating Firm', *British Journal of Management*, 2: 41–50.

—— Robson, M., and Townsend, J. (1987), 'The Size Distribution of Innovating Firms', *Journal of Industrial Economics*, 35: 297–316.

Penrose, E. (1959), *The Theory of the Growth of the Firm* (Basil Blackwell, Oxford).

Reinganum, J. (1982), 'A Dynamic Game of R. & D.: Patent Protection and Competitive Behavior', *Econometrica*, 50: 671–88.

Robson, M., Townsend, J., and Pavitt, K. (1988), 'Sectoral Patterns of Production and Use of Innovations in the UK: 1945–1983', *Research Policy*, 17: 1–14.

Rosenberg, N. (1974), 'Science, Invention and Economic Growth', *Economic Journal*, 84: 90–108.

Salmon, M. (1982), 'Error Correction Mechanisms', *Economic Journal*, 92: 615–29.

Sargent, T., and Sims, C. (1977), 'Business Cycle Modelling without Pretending to Have too much a priori Economic Theory', in C. Sims (ed.), *New Methods in Business Cycle Research* (Federal Reserve Bank of Minneapolis, Minneapolis).

Sawyer, M. (1971), 'Concentration in British Manufacturing Industry', *Oxford Economic Papers*, 23: 352–83.

Scherer, F. M. (1965), 'Firm Size, Market Structure, Opportunity and the Output of Patented Inventions', *American Economic Review*, 55: 1097–125.

—— (1967), 'Research and Development Allocation under Rivalry', *Quarterly Journal of Economics*, 81: 359–94.

—— (1980), *Industrial Market Structure and Economic Performance* (2nd edn., Rand McNally, Chicago).

—— (1982), 'Inter-industry Flows and Productivity Growth', *Review of Economics and Statistics*, 64: 627–34.

—— (1983), 'Concentration, R. & D. and Productivity Change', *Southern Economic Journal*, 50: 221–5.

—— (1984), *Innovation and Growth: Schumpeterian Perspectives* (MIT Press, London).

—— (1992), 'Schumpeter and Plausible Capitalism', *Journal of Economic Literature*, 30: 1416–33.

—— and Ross, T. (1990), *Industrial Market Structure and Economic Performance* (3rd edn., Houghton Mifflin, Boston, Mass.).

Schmalensee, R. (1987), 'Collusion versus Differential Efficiency: Testing Alternative Hypotheses', *Journal of Industrial Economics*, 35: 399–425.

—— (1989), 'Inter-industry Studies of Structure and Performance', forthcoming in R. Schmalensee and R. Willig (eds.), *Handbook of Industrial Economics* (North-Holland; Amsterdam).

Schrieves, R. (1978), 'Market Structure and Innovation: A New Perspective', *Journal of Industrial Economics*, 26: 329–47.

Scott, J., and Pascoe, G. (1987), 'Purposive R. & D. in Manufacturing', *Journal of Industrial Economics*, 36: 193–206.

Shankerman, M. (1991), 'How Valuable is Patent Protection?', mimeo (London School of Economics).

—— and Pakes, A. (1986), 'Estimates of the Value of Patent Rights in European Countries During the Post-1950 Period', *Economic Journal*, 196: 1052–76.

Slater, M. (1980), 'The Managerial Limitation to the Growth of Firms', *Economic Journal*, 90: 520–8.

Smith, I., Tether, B., Thwaites, A., Townsend, J., and Wynarczyk, P. (1993), 'The Performance of Innovative Small Firms', in P. Swann (ed.), *New Technologies and the Firm* (Routledge, London).

Smith, R., and Blundell, R. (1986), 'An Exogeneity Test for a Simultaneous Equation Tobit Model with an Application to Labour Supply', *Econometrica*, 54: 679–85.

Steedman, H., and Wagner, K. (1987), 'Machinery, Production Organization and Skills; Kitchen Manufacture in Britain and Germany', mimeo (National Institute of Economic and Social Research).

Sterlacchini, A. (1989), 'R. & D., Innovations and Total Factor Productivity Growth in British Manufacturing', *Applied Economics*, 21: 1549–62.

Stoneman, P. (1983), *The Economic Analysis of Technological Change* (Oxford University Press, Oxford).

Sullivan, D. (1988), 'Dynamic Oligopoly and the Times Series Properties of Advertising, Sales and the Stock Market Rate of Return in the US Cigarette Industry', mimeo (Northwestern University, Evanston, Ill).

Swann, P. (1993), 'Inference from Mixed Bags: The Economic Value of Patent Counts, Innovation Counts and the Like', mimeo (London Business School).

Townsend, J., Henwood, F., Thomas, G., Pavitt, K., and Wyatt, S. (1981), 'Innovations in Britain since 1945' (Occasional Paper No.16, SPRU, University of Sussex).

Trajtenberg, M. (1989), 'The Welfare Analysis of Product Innovations, with an Application to CAT Scanners', *Journal of Political Economy*, 97: 444–79.

Utterback, J., and Suarez, F. (1993), 'Innovation, Competition and Industry Structure', *Research Policy*, 22: 1–21.

Van Reenen, J. (1993), 'The Creation and Capture of Rents: Wages, Market Structure and Innovation in UK Manufacturing Firms', mimeo (Institute for Fiscal Studies, London).

Vickers, J. (1986), 'The Evolution of Market Structure when there is a Sequence of Innovations', *Journal of Industrial Economics*, 35: 1–12.

Von Hippel, E. (1976), 'The Dominant Role of Users in the Scientific Instrument Innovation process', *Research Policy*, 5: 212–39.

—— (1982), 'Appropriability of Innovation Benefits as a Predictor of the Source of Innovation', *Research Policy*, 11: 95–115.

—— (1988), *The Sources of Innovation* (Oxford University Press, Oxford).

Wallis, K. (1980), 'Econometric Implications of the Rational Expectations Hypothesis', *Econometrica*, 48: 49–73.

Waterson, M., and Lopez, A. (1983), 'The Determinants of R. & D. Intensity in the U.K.', *Applied Economics*, 15: 379–91.

Wenban-Smith, G. (1981), 'A Study of the Movements of Productivity in Individual Industries in the UK, 1968–79', *National Institute Economic Review*, 97: 57–66.

White, H. (1980), 'A Heteroskedasticity—Consistent Covariance Matrix Estimator and a Direct Test for Heteroskedasticity', *Econometrica*, 48: 817–38.

Wickens, M. (1982), 'The Efficient Estimation of Econjometric Models with Rational Expectations', *Review of Economic Studies*, 49: 55–67.

Willman, P. (1991), 'Bureaucracy, Innovation and Appropriability', mimeo (London Business School).

Wu, D. (1973), 'Alternative Tests of Independence Between Stochastic Regressors and Disturbances', *Econometrica*, 41: 733–50.

Index

174   *Index*

export intensity, as factor of monopoly
   49, 51–3, 57–8

food, drink, and tobacco industry 16,
   23, 24, 93

Geroski, P. A.:
   and Jacquemin, A. 111
   and Machin, S. 139
   and Walters, C. 15
Griliches, Z. and Lichtenberg, F. 96
growth, *see* economic growth; industry
   growth; productivity growth; sales
   growth

Hsaio, C., *see* Anderson, T. and Hsaio,
   C.

import intensity:
   as factor of monopoly 48–9, 52–3,
      57–8, 148
   and profitability 110, 113, 114,
      115–17, 120
   and relative performance of
      innovators/non-innovators 135, 137,
      138, 141, 142–3
industrial policy 1–2, 107, 129, 159–61
   creation of 'national champions' 1, 59,
      159
   encouragement for small firms and
      entrants 59, 61–2, 77, 160
   and knowledge flows 107, 160–1
industrial production, relationship to
   innovation output 14–15
industry concentration, and profitability
   110, 113, 114, 115–17
industry growth, and market structure
   49, 51–3, 57–8
industry, sectoral production and use of
   innovation 15–20, 90–107
innovation and innovative activity and
   corporate performance 129–46,
   150–4
   and entry rates 35, 61–77
   industrial policy on 1–2, 59, 107, 129,
      159–61
   and industrial production 14–15
   and level of R & D activity 22–3, 25,
      108–9, 155–6
   and market share 149–50
   and market structure 26–41, 42–59,
      62, 72, 148
   measurement of 6–12, 25, 106
   methodology for studying 4–6
   opportunity cost 44–5
   process or product view 109–10,
      122–6, 132–4, 151

production and use 9–10, 14–20,
   93–7, 105–7, 156–8
and productivity growth 90–107,
   150–1
and profitability 108–28, 131, 133,
   138–43, 152
'propensity to innovate' 47, 49
R & D activity as measure of 6–12
   passim, 35, 46–7
Schumpeterian hypothesis 43–59, 149
sectoral 15–20, 90–107
and size of firm 13, 20–5, 35, 100,
   148, 158
social rate of return 154
and spillovers 102–5, 109, 118, 154–9
and transformation of firm's skills
   122, 130, 133, 145–6, 151, 153
see also R & D activity; Science Policy
   Research Unit Innovations Database
innovations count:
   as measure of innovative activity 6,
      7–8, 11–12, 106
   by SPRU Innovations Database 12–17,
      25
instruments industry 15–17, 18–19, 24,
   101–2, 157
   see also engineering

Jacquemin, A., *see* Geroski, P. A. and
   Jacquemin, A.
Jaffee, A. 155

knowledge flows:
   and economic growth 19–20
   embodied or disembodied 104–5, 118,
      127
   and industrial policy 107, 160–1
   intersectoral 90–107
   see also spillovers

Levin, R. *et al.* 158, 159
Lichtenberg, F., *see* Griliches, Z. and
   Lichtenberg, F.

McCurdy, T., *see* Amemiya, T. and
   McCurdy, T.
Machin, S., *see* Geroski, P. A. and
   Machin, S.
Mansfield, E. 35
market concentration:
   and corporate performance 135, 137,
      138, 141, 142–3
   or deconcentration 26–7, 40–1, 62,
      150
   and innovative activity 62, 72
   model of dynamics of: design 27–32;
      results 32–40
   and monopoly 48–9, 51–3, 57–8